DON'T SAY DUMB SHIT

By Sarah Waters

Dedication

This small piece is dedicated to all that our family once was, the miracle that it currently is, and the future of what it will become. This would not be possible without the encouragement of my husband and the bravery and strength I find from my youngest child. May you know that the depths of your worth are truly found within and that your value is not determined by the actions of others. You are strong, my baby. You have overcome obstacles no one should face and will continue to rise above. I'm proud of you every single moment.

Contents

Chapter 1: The Invitation

Injustice. Betrayal. Tragedy. Loss.

Regardless of upbringing, religion, race, ethnicity, or socioeconomic status, none are immune to the human experience. However, some encounter greater levels of these experiences throughout life due to a variety of circumstances. Our natural inclination, as a society, is to judge. Surely someone is to blame. There must be a cause for every effect. There is. But blame, shame, and guilt do nothing to bring resolution or any consolation during the direst of circumstances. The stones of blame, shame, and guilt must not be cast hastily, for there is always more to the story than meets the eye.

This is my journey, our journey, as a family, through the most unbearable of circumstances. Personally, I consider the topics disclosed part of the last frontier of what is taboo discussion in our culture: adolescent mental health issues, specifically personality disorders, and sibling sexual abuse. Will you judge me and my family? I'm sure you will. I have one request as we move forward together, should you choose to accept this mother's invitation to a trail of tears. Please hold your stones of judgement, or better yet, pile them neatly as a memorial. For you see, much has been lost for each member of my family and for our family as a corporate unit. We are not the same. We will never be the same.

This is reality in one of the rawest forms. It is not intended to embarrass any involved or to place blame. My only goal is to help bring awareness and remove the stigma. This is my desperate attempt to provide companionship to someone else, on what is possibly the loneliest road a mother can travel.

As a parent on this journey, may you find comfort and validation of your thoughts and feelings. There is no right or wrong way to feel. You have a right to every emotion. Although it may seem like it, you are not alone. There are many others hiding in the shadows who know your anguish well. May we come together to provide support for one another, only piling stones in remembrance of who we once were as mothers, fathers, and individuals. The journey encompasses loss, heartbreak, and tragedy; however, through the difficulties, may we be reborn unto a new purpose and rediscover life, love, and laughter.

As a victim, may you know that you are loved, valuable, and worthy of protection. This is not your fault. I repeat, this is not your fault. You did nothing to deserve abuse. You could never do anything to deserve what has happened to you. Speaking out is the most important thing you can do, and if you have not done so, please don't be afraid.

As the one who committed the offense, know that you are loved. Your family loves you, in spite of your actions. However, that does not mean that we should look away or that you are exempt from the consequences what you have done.

As a friend or family member, may you learn some of the common pitfalls to avoid. Yes, you mean well with your comments and suggestions; however, there are times that your thoughts are best left unsaid. May you discover that there are meaningful and practical ways you can help and provide support without overstepping boundaries.

So join me, if you dare. This is your invitation. Gather your own stones of injustice, betrayal, tragedy, loss, grief, and anger. Carry them carefully. The burden is great. Our heavy burdens will become stones of remembrance of what we have lost. Together, we will raise a memorial for past, present, and future survivors. This is *our* story.

Chapter 2: The Last Frontier

Society changes over time. Many things that used to be considered taboo or even profane have diminished or completely transformed over the years. Over the course of history, topics such as sex, domestic violence, illness, and even death have been accepted as part of life. Television commercials continually promote medications for everything from depression, anxiety, frequent urgency, irritable bowel syndrome, to erectile dysfunction. However, there are still topics related to sex, violence, and mental health that are only whispered behind closed doors.

These topics make us uncomfortable. If you are unfortunate enough to discover sibling sexual abuse has occurred in your home, brace yourself. They say it is the worst situation any parent can find themselves in, and it's true. You are the parent to both the victim and the perpetrator. Yes, I used the word perpetrator to describe a child who is old enough to make independent decisions. It is true. Accept it. You are now the parent of a victim who has been horribly violated in the most intimate way possible in the "protection" of their own home, and you are the parent of a child who has committed unspeakable, even monstrous, acts.

You love both fiercely. You would give your very life to make this reality become nothing more than a nightmare that you can awake from. Yet, day after day, you realize that while this is a nightmare, you will never wake up. You are the protector of both. The physical, mental, and emotional welfare of each child is your responsibility. How did this happen? Why our family? What do we do?

Unfortunately, the concept of sibling sexual abuse is generally considered absurd. Many, even those in social services and law enforcement, dismiss the behavior as age-appropriate sexual exploration that is by mutual consent. In some cases, this may be true. However, when one sibling exerts his or her power, or uses coercion, intimidation, or manipulation to engage in sexual activity, it is abuse. To make matters worse for the victim, the abuser may often use threats, intimidation, and/or physical violence to ensure secrecy. As siblings, the victim and perpetrator frequently live under the same roof, making easy access to assault and opportunity to verbally or nonverbally threaten or reinforce previous threats continually. Thus, the cycle continues.

Hopefully, the future will hold some type of support group for parents who are trying to come to terms with the reality of what has occurred in their family. There are online support groups for nearly anything imaginable. Yet, when our lives ended that dreaded evening in September, and I had no idea where to turn or what to do, I found little information at my fingertips concerning sibling sexual abuse. Information abounded concerning incest at the hands of parents, step-parents, aunts, uncles, and older cousins, but there was little concerning siblings. All of the information I found said to report the abuse, seek counseling, and comfort the victim, but there was nothing to tell me what to do or how to survive as a mother. As a parent, I soon realized that I was alone in a sea of despair, confusion, and anger that would not subside for quite some time.

The shame of disclosure holds the victim and their family hostage in the shadows of abuse. Why? Why should we be more ashamed of rape because it occurs at the hands of a sibling and not of a stranger, date, uncle, cousin, or step-parent? These other offenses are "acceptable" to privately discuss; there is a general sense of awareness and support available. But what if the siblings are both female? Isn't that just "normal" sexual exploration? No. Rape is not exclusive to males; females are capable of rape as well. Family sexual abuse is more common than any of us would like to conceive, and sibling sexual abuse falls in that category, although it is generally swept under the rug by parents and many professionals.

Victims can't just "get over it."

Along with this first taboo topic comes mental health issues. Victims of abuse often suffer from depression, anxiety, and Post Traumatic Stress Disorder (PTSD). Victims can't just "get over it." The feelings of depression and anxiety that accompany abuse and disclosure are real. The nightmares are real. The aftermath of abuse requires therapy, reassurance, and compassion. Repression is not the answer. Being "strong" is not the answer. Just forgetting about it and moving on is not the answer. Medication unto zombification is not the answer. PTSD is complex and different for every individual. Regardless of what you have gone through, you do not understand the feelings of the victim. Be supportive by your presence. Ask before giving gentle hugs. And for heaven's sake, don't tell the victim how to feel or what to do in order to get back to normal. The life of the victim has been forever changed. The lives of the parents of the victim have forever changed. We are in this together. We will struggle, but we will become stronger through this. We do not need your commentary of suggestions or judgements. Regardless of how close we may be, you will never know the depth of our pain.

Those who abuse do not necessarily have a mental health issue; however, our oldest daughter struggled for years without diagnosis or proper treatment. Most people who were aware of our struggles tried to chalk it up to teen hormones or some other form of typical behavior. Mental health problems can be hereditary and there was some evidence of potential disorders in previous generations; however, older generations didn't seek help. Their eccentric and abusive behaviors were justified as being provoked, a general reflection of the time, or simply considered, "That's just the way they were." Although family members often suffered mental, emotional, and physical abuse, it was cast aside. After all, it was normal. Right?

The journey to diagnosis of a mental health condition is difficult, especially when dealing with adolescents. Diagnosis, misdiagnosis, or total lack of diagnosis doesn't discredit the experience of living with an individual with a mental health issue or make the condition less real. Parents often have a deep sense when something is awry with a child, even when routine health checks indicate normal development and other more "seasoned" parents surely know what's best in comparison to the inexperience of new parents. When our oldest child first exhibited extreme mood swings at a young age, I was concerned. At times, her behavior was erratic, at best. Yet, her mood swings didn't often lend to physically aggressive behavior at that time, and when it did, there was always a "valid" reason. From the time she could talk, she could lie without hesitation. She wasn't social with children her own age, preferring adults or younger children. She often reported instances of bullying at school, yet when we discussed the issue with teachers, there was no corroboration to her stories. In general, she was a loner. Okay, there isn't anything wrong with that. She's just different. She walks to the beat of her own drum, and in time that will beneficial. When I perceived dissent between siblings, it was easily cast aside as typical sibling rivalry. All the while, I knew that something was "off." I couldn't articulate my concern properly, yet in my heart of hearts, I knew something was terribly wrong and my oldest child's behaviors were not normal; she had the capability to eventually harm someone.

Chapter 3: Isn't It Just Normal Teenage Behavior?

Adolescence is a crazy time. The body experiences tremendous hormonal, psychological, and physiological changes abruptly. Many tweens/teens who were previously calm, docile "angels" become rebellious, aggressive, defiant, disrespectful, anxious, isolated, or depressed. In the midst of all of these changes is a greater awakening to sexuality. Needless to say, these years are often filled with angst and frustration for all members of the family. That's normal.

As an educator, I've always said that the middle school years are some of the most turbulent and that we all deserve a survivor t-shirt for making it to adulthood. Forget the actual academics, just the social atmosphere of moving from an elementary school to a much larger school with triple or quadruple the number of students can be a difficult transition for any child. Which social group should be joined? Don't make the wrong friends or join the wrong crowd. Get good grades. Be involved in sports or some other group at school. Don't get into trouble. Stay out of the drama. Add these issues with the normal tumult of the age and stage, and any family can find themselves with many difficult, emotional evenings often filled with tears, eye rolls, and a general huffy nature of a pubescent mutant.

While the social behavior of our oldest child didn't exactly fit the definition of normal during her elementary school years, she was a good student. The odd behaviors and mood swings exhibited at home were concerning; however, other parents and family members were quick to say it was typical or made excuses. Although their reassurance didn't make me feel any better, I was continually told that all would level out in a few years or that I was concerned over nothing.

By the time we hit the "tween" years, things shifted. The periodic mood swings we were accustomed to from early childhood took a drastic spike. Anger seemed to be the pervading atmosphere. Everything was negative. She didn't like school (although she had exemplary grades) and hated the bus. There was rivalry with "that one girl" at school. She became hateful toward her sister for being younger and didn't want to play anymore; she was too old for that. She became jealous of a neighbor girl who was a few years older, accusing her of "stealing" her little sister from her. At a family event, supervised by other adults, she put a rope around a cousin's neck and attempted to strangle him. We were never able to determine the truth of the matter, as none of the adults in charge were directly supervising. She claimed they were playing a game. When the other children present were questioned, none of the stories matched. Each event concerning her odd behavior was isolated with weeks or sometimes months in-between incidents. In isolation, each could be dismissed as a childhood squabble or misunderstanding. Of course, when things didn't go the way she desired or she was held accountable for her actions with appropriate consequences, we were the devil incarnate. That's typical adolescent behavior, according to most parents. We looked forward to better days ahead when the hormones would even out and a more level headed nature would prevail.

Other than intense mood swings and occasional outbursts of anger and/or tears at home (stomping, door slamming, or throwing clothes across her room), there were no signs of disturbing behavior that could be reported as problematic. Her teachers found her pleasant to work with and more mature than her age. She was often referred to as a "little adult." Yet, in spite of all of her good qualities, I felt a pervading sense of doom and anticipation that something was not right. Her lies became more frequent. She would lie about anything or nothing. She would lie to get what she wanted. She would lie to get out of trouble. Both of these are normal behaviors; however, she would also lie for the sake of lying. I'm not talking about little lies, but great, elaborate stories of her achievements that were simply beyond belief or stories about other children at school in which she was either the victim or the only individual standing up for what was right. When we expressed concern about some of the events that were supposedly happening, we soon learned that there was no truth in it. Of course, her explanation was that she was telling the truth and that the teachers simply didn't pay attention to know what was really going on. There were stories of problems on the bus, but the bus driver wasn't aware of any issues. The continual lying became problematic, but in many cases the stories were quite believable. We couldn't tell where the ounce of truth stopped and the lie began. We knew the truth had to be somewhere in the middle. There simply couldn't be continual problems and drama at school, where everyone was against her and saying horrible things, right in the classroom and on the bus, every day, without anyone noticing anything.

While she talked of friends at school and teachers perceived that she had friends, she was growing more isolated. At this point, she had "crossed off" many of the students she had considered friends from elementary school. They "changed" when they entered middle school and she didn't want anything to do with them. She chose to sit directly behind the bus driver to avoid other students. The tension continually increased between our daughter and another girl she had been friends with since first grade. The other student was climbing the social ladder and leaving our daughter behind. This is part of growing up. Social circles ebb and flow and change throughout school, especially at this age. We all went through the heartache of losing friends and found joy in embracing new friends as we found our niche during the awkward years. Surely this would soon be the case for her as well. We provided comfort and counsel; however, nothing seemed to calm the impending storm.

Finally, I received a phone call at work. It was the assistant principal of her school who was previously a colleague. The conversation was quick and to the point.

I hate to call you at work, but you're daughter has had a problem with "Karen." She's not innocent in this. Today, when she got off the bus, she threatened to kill Karen. Other students heard her say it. Karen's mom is understandably upset and came to the school this morning. We've already spoken with the other students and they say it's true. Your daughter says they are all lying and are against her. She says they hate her. I'm going to refer her for peer mediation with the school counselor to resolve this. I know you are good parents and will deal with this at home, so I'm not going to put this in her file or take disciplinary action.

I'm not the type of parent who believes her baby is incapable of wrong. If my child does wrong, tell me. Now, I had officially been told. When we talked with our daughter, she became very angry and hysterical. She denied everything and claimed that there were no other students around when she allegedly threatened the other student. She yelled her regular battle cries when faced with consequences, "Everyone else is lying! I'm telling the truth! How could you believe that? I didn't do anything wrong! They are all against me!"

Eventually, Karen's mother and I met up at a basketball game. She addressed the issue and was obviously shaken. What could I do but apologize? Even though my child swore her innocence, I knew in my heart this event happened. Karen's demeanor changed toward my daughter. She walked a wide circle and avoided our entire family. Her mother became guarded and distant. They even avoided us in public and would whisper to others as we walked by, "That's the girl who threatened Karen." It was embarrassing.

Our daughter's mood swings became increasingly worse. Her lies, for any reason or no reason, became more frequent. We put her in counseling. Her behavior grew worse over the period of six months. Every week she had a counseling appointment, her behavior was horrid. She would remain angry for days before and after. Obviously, going to counseling intensified her anger and made her mood swings worse. My younger daughter and I walked on egg shells to avoid confrontation every day after school. After several months, we eventually discontinued counseling. It wasn't worth it. Her interactions at school remained stressed, and she insisted that Karen and her mother (a teacher) were continually trying to ruin her life. When we discontinued counseling was the first time she referred to herself in third person. It was dark as we exited the building, she got in the passenger seat of the car, looked at me, and said, "If you *EVER* try to make me go back to counseling again, I'll make sure the *OTHER* "Brittney" comes back." Instantly I felt like I had been duped and was fearful. Her voice was cold and threatening. The school year ended, and over the summer I took a position at a school in a neighboring county. This provided our children the opportunity to change school districts. Surely, this would be a fresh start and prove an end to her social woes.

The new school was a 7-12 facility. Having been in band since 5th grade and previously selected for honor's band, she quickly adapted to a new director over the summer. I felt confident that joining a group would allow her the opportunity to build relationships prior to the start of school; however, the negativity resumed immediately. The only positive discussion involved the director and how superior he was to the director at her previous school. Of course, within days she believed she was the prized pupil, and as a 7th grader, the best flute player in the band who would soon be first chair over upperclassmen. Although she learned names of a few students, none became friends.

Hired as an 8th grade teacher, I was also asked to teach a split class of advanced 7th graders for nine weeks. My daughter was one of the students placed in the class. I was a little nervous to have my own child as a student, as most people perceive that teachers who have their own children show favoritism. I discussed this with her before school started. I made a point to let her know that she would be treated like every other student, and that above all else I would be fair. She would earn her grade just like every other student.

She was a quiet student. In a group of incessantly chatty middle schoolers, she was hardly noticeable. She kept to herself. She always had a book and read at the beginning of every class and any time her work was complete. She wasn't the most successful at group work, but participated more as she grew to know other students. Only in the classroom environment did symptoms of anxiety appear. She was a frequent nail biter, face picker, and hair twirler. No other teacher had discussed symptoms of anxiety, so I assumed it was due to the change of environment. It didn't subside.

The following year, she was my student for an entire semester. I noticed the symptoms of anxiety continued. She had seemingly made a couple friends, although she had no interaction with them outside of school. It wasn't long until she began to complain about the few friends that she had. Either they were joining the wrong crowd and doing bad things on the weekend or were part of the "sporty" group and were snotty toward anyone who was not a part of extracurricular sports. She withdrew more. She began to spend a substantial amount of time in Mrs. K's room before and after school. Sometimes it was for tutoring, but it mostly served as her social interaction.

I noticed that her behavior during small group assignments had changed from the previous year. Instead of being more laid back, she often asserted herself as the leader. At first, this seemed like a good thing. Perhaps she was coming into her own; however, her leadership skills resembled a dictator. Her way was the best way. If the entire group wanted to go in a different direction, she would attempt to branch off from the group and do the entire project herself. She was going to do it "right" and they were not going to get her grade. But sometimes her way was completely opposed to the directions. In one small research project, she argued with her partner and insisted that they do things her way. As I made my way around the room, I noticed that they were on a website that wouldn't yield results. I pointed this out to her, and my daughter informed me that I was incorrect and she knew what she was doing. The other student commented, "I've been trying to tell her we were on the wrong site, but she won't go to any of the websites suggested or let me touch the computer." Again, I redirected the instruction and reviewed the directions, as I would with any other student. But according to my child, I was wrong and she was right. Why argue with a teacher who created the assignment and spent hours searching the web for the best resources? This is only one example. The accounts of other students and teachers being wrong, stupid, lazy, and irresponsible in comparison to her own superior work ethic and morals go on forever.

During this time, she began to pursue a number of unhealthy relationships with adults. She would choose an adult to befriend; gender made no difference. This individual would be her confidant. While most teenagers need someone to trust and talk to about typical teen angst, her relationships quickly became unbalanced, obsessive, and filled with deceit and manipulation. She would build each relationship and push the boundaries of confidence until any responsible adult would eventually express concern to the parents.

A typical case would begin with the discussion of school drama, the immorality of her peers, or a dislike of math. Over time, the topics would shift to not getting along with her little sister or dislike of the neighbor girl who was slightly older, we expected too much of her, and the stress of teenage life was more than she could handle. She didn't know how much longer she could take it. For some, this last, on-going, "I don't know how much more I can take." was enough alarm to warrant parental discussion. When veiled threats of self-harm were not enough, the lies skyrocketed to new levels indicating a need for medical attention and our refusal to take her to the hospital because our insurance wouldn't cover costs. This became frequent, with multiple individuals, ranging from family, friends, teachers, and clergy from three states contacting us with their concerns. Out of concern for our daughter, they were kind enough to forward the text messages or e-mails. When we would question our daughter, she claimed that she didn't ever say those things. When presented with physical evidence, she didn't know how it got there or went into hysterics about how we didn't trust her and were always looking over her shoulder. One by one, she built a relationship with an adult, pressed it to the breaking point, and then dropped each one like a hot potato because they had betrayed her or we had "taken" that person from her by "spying" on her private conversations when they expressed concern and sent us screen shots of the messages. It was impossible to completely restrict her access to technology. Although we could limit her access at home, we could not police her activity on school devices or if she used a friend's device to e-mail someone during band practice.

Thankfully, every adult she befriended was a trustworthy individual who looked out for her well-being and alerted us to concerns, instead of finding someone online who would take advantage of a teen girl. These relationships culminated into what became the most obsessive with Mrs. K, during. She would message Mrs. K at all hours of the day and night with veiled hints of self-harm, her hatred for us as parents, or an urgent need to speak with her immediately because she didn't know what she was going to do. The obsession grew progressively over the course of a year, until Mr. K finally came to me personally. He also had her in class and had seen concerning behaviors. His personal experiences with our daughter, coupled with the incessant harassment of his wife, made him exceptionally concerned. While we knew that she occasionally messaged Mrs. K for homework help or to simply stay in touch, we had no idea what had transpired. He gave me examples of messages and times sent. Although we did not allow technology in the bedroom at night to hopefully ensure a full night's rest, she would sneak her iPod at all hours to send frantic messages to Mrs. K and others well after mid-night into the wee hours of the morning. Discussion of her behavior toward Mrs. K resulted in the typical hysterics. As a family, we walked on egg shells all the time now, never knowing what mood she might be in or what could potentially set her off.

We noticed changes in her sexual behavior. She wasn't interested in boys, even when a few flirted with her. She claimed that those interested were either beneath her academically, were jerks, or were part of the "sporty" group. She talked of the increase of sexually active, bisexual, and homosexual students. She would talk badly about anyone in her age group who was in a relationship, regardless of sexual orientation. She was judgmental of anything remotely sexual, including swimsuits or what other people wore during gym class. While I was thankful she was modest, I was alarmed at the harshness she displayed toward anyone or anything who didn't meet her strict moral standard. Her personal beliefs were extreme and not a reflection of what was taught at home. She frequently drew thick lines between herself and others with statements that often started with, "I would never…", "I can't believe s/he does/wears that and is a Christian…", or "I thought she was different like me, but now…"

While she spoke poorly of those who were engaging in sexual behaviors, her own actions didn't adhere to her own moral compass. Once, at our home, I witnessed her aggressively attempt to kiss an older girl, who obviously tried to get away. On another occasion, a family friend saw her inappropriately touch the girl's breasts, but then laugh it off in jest. Our youngest daughter complained that she would walk in on her while showering or in her bedroom while changing, stare, and refuse to leave.

One afternoon, I heard "Stop it! Don't touch me!" come from my youngest daughter's bedroom. Using my best ninja-mom skills, I approached quickly and quietly enough to catch the oldest in bed with her. My younger daughter was obviously afraid, while her sister didn't flinch at my presence or move away from her sister's body, which was in a full embrace from behind. Like any good parent, I had a fit! With each in separate bedrooms, I told my younger daughter that I would speak with her sister first, but I saw what happened and wanted her full story. By this time, we were used to the rules of engagement. When anything happened between siblings, if we didn't speak with the oldest first, she accused us of automatically taking her sister's side before we ever heard the truth. Hearing her side first was a way of appeasing her and attempting to keep the peace. We had learned the hard way to never sit them down together to discuss a fall-out. We had a firm discussion. I was given a tall-tale by my oldest that made no logical sense, yet she showed no remorse or even the slightest hint of guilt for her inappropriate behavior. My younger daughter downplayed the event. We discussed boundaries, personal space, and what to do when someone made her feel uncomfortable. This fell under the category of normal teen exploration, right? We made extra effort to not allow them to be together unsupervised. Even though I was frequently exhausted from an autoimmune condition, naps were no longer an option unless my husband was home. And bedrooms were private spaces – do not enter your sister's room for any reason, period.

I couldn't shake sense of dread and impending crisis that had pervaded my soul. Something was wrong. My oldest daughter had become increasingly aggressive, although not overtly aggressive according to many standards. One day she had been caught in another lie. I allowed her time to cool off before entering her room to discuss her behavior. My husband was at work, but we spoke about the incident and decided the consequences for yet another falsehood. I went to discuss her behavior, the importance of telling the truth, and lay out the consequences for the offense. She was seething. I had never encountered her so defiant and filled with complete rage when I was explaining things as calmly as I could. She didn't show any remorse for lying, only hatred for being found out. Since she refused to discuss what had happened, I told her I was sorry that she was upset, but there were consequences for her behavior. She was grounded.

When I stood to leave her room, she rose behind me. I could hear her breathing. My back was to her, but I could feel the tension in the room like an unseen force. My pulse quickened, the hair stood on the back of my neck, and I knew she was contemplating personal attack. Knowing the only advantage I had was weight, as she is taller and physically stronger, I had nothing to defend myself with other than words. In my best authoritative voice, trying to mirror confidence, I informed her that if she was thinking of jumping on me, that although she might be taller and stronger, but my butt was larger and heavier. If she became physically violent toward me, I would find a way to restrain her until 911 arrived to take her away. She didn't budge. I left the room and called my husband to fill him in on the incident. He didn't know what to say, other than he was glad nothing serious had happened. I was officially afraid of my child.

Friends and family members said her behavior was normal. After all, she hadn't actually committed any act of violence and it could be much worse; I should be thankful she was "such a good girl." Seemingly, she was a good girl, but something was amiss. Knowing that our opportunity to get help for whatever was going wrong was running out, as she only had a few years left at home before she turned 18, we took her to the doctor. Maybe she had some sort of hormonal or chemical imbalance that could be the root of her aggressive behavior. We didn't know, but it seemed to be the next logical step. The doctor's appointment was dramatic. She hated us. How dare we make her get bloodwork? She tried to refuse, but the nurse was eventually able to persuade her into cooperation. (God bless nurses.) The doctor recommended counseling, and we agreed to give it another shot. Instead of taking her to the local family center, it was suggested that we take to her for a full evaluation and see an adolescent specialist. Hoping for answers, we agreed and made the weekly, bi-weekly, and eventually monthly trek two hours after school for her appointments. I was determined to find an answer and something that could help stabilize her mood.

All results of lab work returned normal. The only diagnosis provided from the psychological evaluation was mild depression and anxiety; however, due to her responses during testing that shed an overly positive light on herself, a personality disorder was suspected. We continued counseling so she could learn proper communication and coping skills to deal with her emotions. This was a long, tedious, and in spite of insurance, a very costly venture. But it had to help, right? Someone would find answers. That's their job! With minimal results over several months, the psychologist eventually referred us to a psychiatrist to explore the possibility of a low dose medication to stabilize her mood. Although we were a little fearful of medication possibly increasing depression, we kept the appointment.

We arrived at the psychiatrist's office, our daughter surly as ever on the trip. After some time in the waiting area, she was invited to speak with the psychiatrist first. By the time we were welcome, she had convinced him that she was in total control of her emotions, counseling had helped her tremendously, she had learned coping skills, and her involvement in a youth group and regular devotional time had greatly helped her. She didn't want or need any type of medication. She no longer felt depressed or anxious and had no idea why we thought differently. Much to our surprise, the doctor was quick to indicate that if she felt that she didn't need the medication, there was no need to prescribe it. The patient had to have a certain level of "buy in" in order for any type of therapy to continue.

Clearly, she had won. At her request and indication of buy in from the psychiatrist, we discontinued all therapy sessions while we prayed for a miracle, knowing we only had two years until she graduated high school. We could hold on that long and keep anything bad from happening for two more years. We had made it this far. If we had only known the truth that had been ongoing in the shadows, we could have prevented the worst days, weeks, and months of our lives. The bomb was ticking. We were oblivious of the level present danger and violence in our home.

Chapter 4: The Intermission

For a brief time, it seemed that her moods were more subdued. The neighbor girl, who was the cause of much jealously, moved away. We moved to a different church, providing a new opportunity for her to make friends and to locate another confidant to pursue; however, she took a new approach this time and desired to impress her mentors with her spiritual maturity and adult conversations, instead of exaggerated drama and fabricated stories. Was she really starting to grow up? Were things improving? We dared to hope.

She attended two summer church camps, one as a camper and the other as a worker. She returned home with a new career path. No longer did she want to pursue horse training, but instead, she declared a call to children's or youth ministry. She wanted to be re-baptized as a symbol of her new call to the faith and desire to move forward spiritually. She was actively engaged in church services and volunteered to help with the children's class. She wanted to spend time with us and seemed happier.

Meanwhile, over the course of several months, our younger daughter had grown more isolated at home. She often seemed depressed and exhibited some symptoms of anxiety. Even her appearance and choice of clothing changed. She went from wearing sparkly "girly" clothes and dresses to wearing gym apparel, plain colors, and loosely fitted clothing. She continually sported a pony tail, taking no real interest in her hair or general appearance. Most girls go through the "grunge" phase of adolescence; I was certain this was the case. When she occasionally complained of discomfort in her ankles, knees, and wrists, I assumed it was a symptom of growing pains. This too shall pass.

I should have paid closer attention to the hints that I didn't know were hints. The demeanor of our youngest was completely different when her sister was not present. Instead of fading into the shadows, she was her normal, bubbly self. Why could I not see that there was something much more sinister than mean older sister moments and a domineering personality? How many times had she tried to tell me what her sister was doing to her? How many times did I unknowingly enable the perpetrator? Why didn't I see the writing on the wall? When she questioned the sincerity of her sister's new spiritual transformation, I too expressed concern, but we could not judge the heart of another, and time would tell of her transformation. The bomb was ticking and near detonation.

Chapter 5: The Bomb

Silent tears, incredible silence, and awkward tension….a nodding of the head, "Yes."

Depending on the type of bomb, a small change in atmosphere can trigger an explosion. Our oldest daughter's new spiritual high proved to be the trigger. We were all buying the new and improved version she presented. Her sister, knowing the truth of the dual life she lived must have been sickened at the charade. I can only imagine the horror of watching your parents believe a liar, knowing that she is capable of unspeakable acts, and that by entering ministry with young people in the church, she only creates a future pool of victims for years to come.

Our younger daughter became increasingly upset, she didn't sleep well or eat normally, she frequently complained of not feeling well, suffered nightmares, and appeared depressed. When she arranged a movie night with her godfather, it wasn't unusual. He would occasionally take the girls on "Uncle Matt" days to see a movie of their choice. When he came to pick her up for the second day in a row, I assumed she was finally getting things off her chest. I knew of some drama at school. Maybe she just didn't want to talk to me about it.

Knowing that something was clearly amiss, he sat with her in the driveway after arriving home. She was sullen, withdrawn, and obviously had something heavy to get off her mind, yet she wouldn't talk. Feeling the severity of the situation, he asked a series of questions that revealed the truth.

The next day, he let me know that we needed to talk soon. I could tell by urgency of his voice and the firm look in his eye that this was serious. That Sunday, after getting together to celebrate my birthday with friends, I rode back with him to get the scoop. At that moment, our lives changed forever.

"What's up? This seems serious."
"It is. I don't know how to say this, so I'm just going to say it I guess."
"Okay. You know I'd rather you just tell it to me straight anyway."

"Well, you know I took her out the other night and that she's been pretty upset."

"Yeah."

"It's her sister. She's been abusing her for quite some time now."

Silence.

"I know it's true. I can feel it in my bones. Her demeanor when we were talking…you can't make that stuff up. I knew something was really wrong, and she wouldn't talk, so I started asking a few questions."

"Is it a problem at school?"

"No."

"Is it your parents?"

"No."

"Is it something at home?"

"Yes."

"Is the problem with your sister?"

"Yes."

"Is she hurting you?"

Deathly silence and awkward tension…."Yes."

"I knew the next question I had to ask. I didn't want to ask. I didn't want to make this more awkward than it was or for you to think I was asking an inappropriate question or anything like that. What's worse, is I knew the answer before I asked."

"Is it sexual?"

Silent tears, incredible silence, and awkward tension….a nodding of the head, "Yes."

They didn't discuss the details because it was too raw and seemed inappropriate at the moment to ask anything further. The only details that emerged were that it had been ongoing for two years and that violence and restraint were involved. She didn't want us to know. She didn't want us to be mad that she told. She thought our knowing would end our new happiness of her sister's sudden transformation. She didn't want to upset anyone. She begged him not to tell, but he explained that we had to know, we would believe her, we would protect her no matter what, she didn't do anything to cause or deserve this, and that she was absolutely right to tell. She was brave. He didn't know what would happen next or what would have to happen, but the abuse would never happen again. We would figure this out together.

Our entire family changed that day. The dynamics would never be the same. The bomb exploded. My mind swirled with questions. What do I do? How will I tell my husband when I get home? Where do we get help? How do we ensure safety? What happens now?

When we arrived home, I had to act as if everything was fine. Our friend, "Uncle Matt" sat in the living room while the girls did their own thing and eventually selected something from Netflix. I cornered my husband privately and told him the horrible reality. He sat in shock. He was angry. We wanted to storm out of the room and confront our oldest child with what we knew, but we didn't. Our youngest was deathly afraid that her sister would kill her when she found out she told. Little did we know that fear wasn't irrational.

I went to the room of our youngest and sat with her for a long time. We hugged and cried. I think I cried more than she did. I assured her that we loved her, we believed her, and that this would never happen again. It wasn't her fault. She didn't do anything to deserve this. There was never anything she could do to deserve to have someone hurt her like that. I apologized for not knowing sooner. She wanted to know what would happen next. I didn't have an answer. Her biggest concern was that we not tell her sister. "Once she knows, Mom, I can't live here anymore. I won't be safe. She WILL KILL ME!" I promised to keep her and the secret safe from her sister.

As the movie played the background, everything became a blur. I have no idea what movie they watched or any conversations that were had. I sat on my phone, numb and angry, trying to keep my composure, while searching for help. How could this happen to us? What did we do wrong? I found an anonymous, online chat hotline for sexual abuse. The lady I spoke with provided numbers for Women's Aid in Crisis, the hotline to report abuse, and told me I needed to call my local CPS. Duh. I knew that, but the reality of shock took away the ability to think and process information. All of this is happened in my little corner of the couch, as shock transformed into the reality of how our lives were about to change. I sat there while the movie played; life looked "normal" at our little house.

There we were, our entire family together watching a movie and having snacks for the last time.

Anger, shame, guilt, and total humiliation at the thought of telling what I knew and the additional details that my daughter disclosed to me that day flooded my thoughts and emotions. I was every emotion and no emotion. Anger and love both originate in the heart and serve a similar function; I would provide protection and find help for both children at any cost.

It was Sunday. Shock impeded my ability to think. Not once did I think to call the police at that moment. There was no rest that night. My husband slept in the floor in front of our youngest daughter's door, just to be sure she was okay. I thought about what had happened, imagined every scenario, and rethought every conversation and text message that could have hinted that there was abuse happening in my own home, yet I had remained oblivious. My anger built. The next day was a holiday and my husband was off. He maintained the appearance of normalcy at home and entertained the kids while I barricaded in the bedroom to make a series of phone calls that would take hours.

Let the phone marathon begin! After taking a few deep breaths, I called the hotline to report abuse. Every word I spoke fell like lead. Although I had spent the entire night thinking of what to say and how to say it, hearing the words come out of my mouth to a total stranger drove home the reality of what had occurred. I choked on sobs and my whole body shook. The operator took the statement, was empathetic, and offered support. She said that once I called CPS, action would take place to remove my oldest child from the home. This would be swift action (24-48 hours) to keep everyone safe. I wasn't surprised by this, but it was a lot to process mentally and emotionally. When I gave my county of residence, so they could assist in moving things forward, there was a sigh, pause, and then an apology. It seems that the county we live in is notorious for not taking swift action when this type of thing occurs. She warned me that it may be a bumpy ride and provided additional resources through Women's Aid in Crisis.

I called CPS. I was transferred a few times and finally found someone who took my statement. She was mechanical. No empathy. No concern. How can anyone listen to the detailed horrors I described of sexual abuse with objects, beating, punching, and restraint to a child and not have any emotion? I'm all for remaining professional, but be a human being. She listened to everything and calmly informed me that it was out of their league; this was a matter for the police and provided the number.

I called the police and was transferred to a state trooper in our home county who took my statement. He told me that what had happened was horrible, but that it was a matter for CPS, not the police. I told him of my previous conversation and referral to police for action to be taken. He said he would follow up with CPS, speak to the prosecuting attorney, and call us back within a couple days. A couple days – 48 hours. We would have to continue the charade for another 48 hours.

Frustrated, angry, and confused, I called Women's Aid in Crisis and spoke with my first real hero, Renée. She listened intently, allowed me to cry, yell, and be the entire mess of emotions I was at the moment. She gave practical advice as to how to deal with my child, the victim; she also stressed the importance of maintaining the appearance of normalcy to my oldest for the sake of safety. She reassured me that I was doing the right thing for both of my children by contacting the authorities and taking actions to remove my oldest child from the home.

"It's has to be this way. Your youngest MUST be your first priority! You are making the most difficult decision any parent can be faced with, and you are making the right one. You are brave, and if every parent responded the way you are, much abuse would be stopped. You are doing the right thing." She gave me the number for HOPE, Inc. and said that they could provide a host of services for the victim and our family in the days, weeks, months, and years ahead. "You have taken the first step toward healing."

The next day, nothing happened. I allowed our youngest to stay home from school and provided a parental note that she was sick. I'm sure she truly felt ill. I know I was literally sick from the mental and emotional rollercoaster. I took the oldest to school and life looked normal to the outside. I taught mechanically. Every time the phone rang in my classroom, I was afraid it would be someone in the main office telling me my oldest child was being taken away that moment. But I didn't hear back from CPS or the police at all that day. The only return call I received was unexpected; it was Renée wanting to see how we were doing, what had happened, and if I had called HOPE yet.

As I entered the beginning of the end of the 48 hour wait time, I was increasingly anxious. Would CPS show up at school and take our oldest away? Would the police come to take a more official statement? Because of the level of violence, would she be arrested? Would she become hysterical and violent when confronted with the truth? How would I explain this to the other students? What would my co-workers think?

Surely, something would happen at the close of the 48 hour period. Nothing. I eventually received a call from my husband that totally shook my world. The police officer had spoken with the prosecuting attorney and returned our call. It seemed that our options were few. They could charge both of our children with incest, in which case both would be removed from the home. We could attempt to sign our oldest over to the state, but because she hadn't been in trouble previously, it may be denied. Of course, they could charge us with neglect and endangerment. However, since we were self-reporting, the officer advised the prosecuting attorney against this. He believed that we really didn't know until the disclosure. He continued explaining their "policy" concerning consent between adolescents, which made the official "dumb shit" list. I was beyond angry. I called CPS back, surely they were going to do something. I received the same response as before; it was not their issue. Our case was quickly kicked out of the system. We didn't fit the mold of what constituted abuse because there were not six years of age between our children. Help was not on the way. We would have to figure this out on our own.

Chapter 6: Finding HOPE

Clearly, the powers that be had failed our family. Our circumstance didn't meet the criteria for abuse. CPS canned our file. The police were no help. Every system designed to help families in crisis failed. We were asked the same questions repeatedly.

"You mean you didn't know this was happening in your home?"

"Why do you think your youngest would say this?"

Sure, I knew our kids weren't best friends and that the older sister was often mean to the younger, but aren't most to an extent? It's not like the logical thought process of raising teen girls goes from sibling rivalry, mean looks, occasional hateful words, alongside the day-to-day normal activities to violent sexual abuse that could have resulted in death!

Desperate for help, I followed the lead and called HOPE, Inc. A Task Force on Domestic Violence. I met my second hero, Kim. Kim listened to my story. She was heartbroken at our tragedy and outraged at how every system intended to provide help failed. She provided support, individual counseling opportunities for each of us, family counseling, and helped me realize what I already knew. If the agencies designed to help were not going to do anything, I must be my own advocate and find help. There had to be help for our family. There had to be help for both of our children! She provided names of additional resources and helped me make phone calls to save time. By the end of the day, I had spoken to numerous acute care facilities. My husband and I decided that it was in the best interest of our family to take our oldest child for a full psychological evaluation.

I discretely took the next day off work, but got up as if it would be a normal day. When it was time to go to school, we sat our oldest daughter down, confronted her with what we knew, and explained what was going to happen that day. She exploded. I comforted our other daughter and made arrangements for her to be picked up shortly. We drove nearly two hours to the closest facility. Indeed, it was the same location where she previously had counseling and refused additional care. Perhaps this was a mistake, but given the limited resources in our area, it was one of our only choices. In order to have her evaluated, we had to go through the emergency room at the adjoining hospital. The nurses were empathetic and assured us that something would be done. They too were in shock that the abuse had been reported to CPS and the police without any results. Within a few hours we were told that she would be admitted for evaluation on the adolescent mental health ward. We spent a total of nine hours in the ER that day, waiting for a bed to be prepared. It was more than a little frustrating when we realized that she was the second patient on the ward. The journey we hoped would bring healing for our family and mental/emotional stability for our oldest began.

She spent five days in a facility unequipped to deal with sexual misconduct. If she had been on drugs or attempted to self-harm, they would have been able to provide assistance. Intake questions and the conversations that followed were the worst. I realize they are professionals with a job to do; however, some of the questions and statements were insensitive at best, and the majority made the "dumb shit" list. During the five days of her stay in acute care, no individual counseling concerning what occurred was provided. No services were suggested that would transition her to another facility, even though we asked for a referral to a residential facility specializing in adolescents who were involved in sexual acts. They kindly collected our insurance money and we ran the roads daily, making arrangements for our youngest, so we could visit our oldest and attend mandatory family counseling sessions with a professional who wasn't regularly on the ward and knew nothing of our case. The mandatory family counseling couldn't be scheduled around my work hours, so I took another day off work for the following conversation:
"Would you like to discuss why you are here with your parents?"
"No."
"Well, okay then. I guess that's it."
Really? Did we just drive two hours for that? You've got to be kidding me!

Thankfully, Kim, from HOPE, Inc. stepped in when the medical profession provided no assistance. Because of her efforts, there was help. Together, we searched for a transition service in-state while we searched for a residential facility that could work with our insurance. Immediately after leaving the acute care facility, our oldest entered a 10 day crisis, outpatient, counseling center. My husband's family literally lives across the road and my parents lived oven an hour away from the counseling center. Our oldest couldn't return home, so "Uncle Matt" stepped in once again. This time, he provided a place for her to stay and met my husband every morning so he could take her to the center. After work, he waited until the daylong session was over and picked her up. Our insurance wouldn't touch this service at $300 a day. Thankfully, they agreed to take payments. During the intake interview at the crisis center, she tripped up in her web of lies. She made a mistake that would prove pivotal in unraveling part of the truth; however, being the master of deceit and manipulation that she is, she kept them perplexed for several days. They eventually realized what she valued most was power and control. Finally, on day nine, she declared her constant hatred and jealously for her sister and confessed to all of the sexual abuse but not strangulation. The psychiatrist indicated that he believed a personality disorder, possibly Borderline Personality Disorder (BPD), could be the root of the issue; however, that decision would not be made lightly. This was progress, so we agreed to additional treatment. By the end of day 14, they said that she was taking too much of their time away from group sessions, she had completely shut down, and they could no longer help her. She clearly needed intense, residential treatment that they could not provide.

Again, Kim remained diligent in the background. She helped me contact Kidlink Treatment Services, a network of specialized residential treatment facilities. Our case was taken by John. Within a few days, I was meeting with him to discuss treatment facilities and provide the necessary paperwork for him to go to work on our behalf. He was thorough and professional, yet compassionate and authentically concerned. He brought a list of facilities that specialize with adolescent sexual perpetrators, with or without adjudication, and had a female ward. Do you have any idea how hard those places are to find? There are few to begin with, and even less that are within a reasonable driving distance from our state. John made his primary and secondary recommendations, based on the success rate of the programs and driving distance. He felt the best fit was in Tennessee. If that didn't work out with the insurance company, the next was Alabama or Texas. While John went to work with the residential facility in Tennessee, we went to work with our insurance company to get a case manager. Within a few days, our case manager in West Virginia set us up with a case manager in Tennessee, Adam, another hero. The ball was rolling. During this transition, our oldest moved in with my parents for twenty-five days, while we waited for insurance clearance and an opening at the facility. We thought we were fortunate; it could have been months. The few facilities that provide this type of specialized care have waiting lists.

So much happened during all of the transition. While we were working to locate a facility for one child, we were taking the other to weekly counseling through HOPE, Inc., and waiting for an appointment with a specialist a month later. Our case was re-opened after the partial confession at the crisis counseling center, and our youngest had to undergo a forensic interview with the state police. Doctor's appointments, a diagnosis of PTSD for the youngest, medication, and school work through homebound services kept the calendar full. Our oldest attended weekly counseling while staying with my parents.

The emotional roller coaster post disclosure is full of unexpected twists, turns, stops, and sometimes goes backwards without warning. The ride is anything but smooth. That's the nature of the recovery process. It's normal. As a result of the stress, I began having intense anxiety attacks and had to have fast acting medication in order to function. Several times I found myself locked in the faculty bathroom, back against the wall, choking on sobs, and trying to concentrate on my breathing so I could teach another class. I was falling apart while trying to function on auto-pilot.

Through it all, well-intentioned people who were aware of the situation said insensitive things. I know they didn't mean to be so crass, but at times it was just too much. When friends and family were unable or unwilling to provide support, those who were little more than strangers stepped up to the plate and helped us maintain what little shred of sanity was left. HOPE, Inc. truly provided hope that there was help and healing for both of my children and our family. The consoling voice over the phone provided a sense of friendship in the depths of despair, without judgement, condemnation, or pity. Kim provided validation, support, encouragement, and sound advice at every turn. She sent regular text messages or made follow up phone calls around my work schedule. I'm not sure how I would have made the journey without her in my cheering section. Clearly, this was not just her job, but a calling.

Chapter 7: Don't Say Dumb Shit

Dumb shit. Don't be offended; there is no better description. Throughout our descent into hell, the comments, judgements, accusations, insinuations, and unsolicited opinions of others was constant. The statements made were inconsiderate, dumb, and hurtful. Just like a pile of horse manure must be removed from a stall for the sake of the animal, the smelly crap load had to be removed from our minds and hearts in order to maintain any hope of stability. At every step, we found ourselves defending our positon as parents and our youngest daughter as a victim.

Why is the victim to blame? I'm not sure why outsiders try to blame the victim, but I am certain that this mentality is what hinders the majority of victims from speaking out. I don't know how anyone could question the validity of the crime perpetrated against my child, especially when the horrific details of the abuse and violence emerged. Nonetheless, I fought as a fierce mother bear. This was not the time to get between me and the ability to protect my little cub. I didn't care who you were or what the situation was, I would fight and win to protect my child at all costs. Part of this fight is dealing with what I affectionately call the dumb shit. We were in the most difficult situation imaginable, yet people made the most hurtful comments, and I was supposed to smile and handle it all with grace and dignity.

At times, sarcasm is my second language, and if I'm not careful, I'll roll my eyes and tell exactly what I think, without ever saying a word. Judge me by my thoughts and raw emotions if you dare, but unless you have walked my path, remember to place those stones in memorial before you attempt to hurl them at my head. These are the real statements of imbeciles, professional and the well-meaning. The responses in italics indicate what I wish I had said, but I found myself speechless.

Professional Dumb Shit

One of the most frustrating aspects of this type of tragedy is the repetition of details. Each professional must hear the story for themselves. As a secondary victim in this situation, it doesn't take long to become fatigued in repeating what has happened and the detailed history of past issues that should have sounded the alarm that help was needed. However, the organizations that we thought would prove helpful were not. In fact, some of the professionals we met along the way caused more emotional harm than good. I know they have a job to perform and some of the questions and statements are par for the course; however, it doesn't change the impact of the words on the mind and heart of a devastated mother. Some of the questions are simply outrageous.

All sexual behavior is learned. Where do you think she learned this? Do you allow your children to view porn?

Well, let's see here. My child is 16. She attends public school. She has had health class providing textbook knowledge, as well as street knowledge of sex from her peers. She was part of band when sexuality became a huge focus, students were passing soft porn they had written through the class, and others were making out in the storage room known as the "dungeon" while the director sat in the office. Once, she walked into the locker room to find six girls in various stages of undress engaged in sexual activity. Was she exposed to porn outside of the reading materials passed during class? Not on my watch. Not knowingly. Do we allow our children to view porn? Are you serious? Do people actually do that? It sounds like families sit down and watch it together like a sitcom! No, we don't.

One of the worst statements made came from the previously mentioned officer who returned our call, after he spoke with the prosecuting attorney.

In 100% of the cases we investigate between the ages of 11 and 16, we find that it is ALWAYS consensual.

Lucky for this officer, my husband was home to receive the call. Maybe I would have held my tongue as he did, sitting in shock at the news, but I doubt it.

First of all, Sir, did you hear anything we said to you? Did you actually write down the graphic details of sexual abuse and restraint? How many cases have you investigated? What do you mean 100% and always consensual? How is having your arm twisted behind your back while being shoved on a bed consensual? How is being restrained by your arms and legs, while having foreign objects shoved into your vagina consensual? How is being punched in the stomach when you cry, don't comply, or try to get away consensual? More details about abuse and violence have surfaced since we spoke. She was choked with a scarf on more than one occasion. The last time she nearly blacked out. She described what it was like. How is being choked to the point of seeing black spots consensual? Doesn't this new information matter? It should, because in our state there is a specific law concerning strangulation. Doesn't that matter? Please, explain this to me!

It continued with our options:

We can charge both children with incest. In that case, both would become wards of the state. You can sign your oldest child over to the state, but we can't guarantee that they would accept her. It's not like she's been in other legal trouble. The prosecuting attorney mentioned charging you with endangerment and neglect, but I assured him that I believed you when you said you didn't know until now.

These are not options. We are not losing our children! How could anyone suggest taking the victim away, as if she's done something wrong in the first place? Oh wait...that 100% of the time, all cases are consensual crap. I remember. The victim is surely to blame somehow. She asked for it right? She wanted to participate in being violently assaulted and wanted to be choked to death. Of course, that's it.

The second option is equally horrid. We don't want to throw our oldest child away! We contacted you to get help! Now help us! Help us! Help us! Can you hear me? Are we speaking the same language? Does your elevator go to the top floor? What does the fact that she hasn't been in other legal trouble have to do with anything? Are you saying that if she had been doing drugs or shoplifted you could help?

Charge us with endangerment and neglect? We reported as soon as we found out and have been rattling every cage in hell trying to get help. I'm glad you believe us and we aren't being charged with anything. I guess that's something for which we can be thankful.

He wished us luck in finding answers to what happened between the girls, since there was no evidence of abuse. (A physical examination was not required because of the time that elapsed since the last occurrence of abuse. However, an exam in the months that followed would corroborate the allegations.)

This encounter left us feeling helpless. First, CPS wouldn't help, claiming it was the job of the police, and now the police wouldn't even investigate. You've got to be kidding me. What were we supposed to do now? The two top agencies that were to provide immediate assistance failed miserably. Not only did they not help, they insinuated time and time again that somehow we were to blame, the victim was to blame, and that the perpetrator must have a reason to have done this, IF in fact, it was abuse. If – such a tiny word with the power to cripple those who have been victimized.

With no help from law enforcement and our case disregarded by CPS, we had to look for alternative solutions. Counselors and other professionals suggested we check with adolescent mental health facilities, given her previous issues and the recent discovery of abuse and violence. A residential facility would be able to provide counseling, therapy, a diagnosis, and treatment. I was given a couple leads to facilities that might be able to provide some sort of assistance. There are very few mental health facilities in our state, and when searching for a place that can provide care for a female who is a perpetrator, the options quickly evaporated.

I started making calls to the few options we had.

Facility Option 1: "No. We can't take her on our unit. She would be a danger to the other girls who are younger. Are you sure she isn't on drugs or something? There are lots of options if she is doing drugs. Try calling option two. "

I completely understand; patient safety is paramount. Are drugs the only explanation for bad behavior? Thanks for the tip; I'll try option two. This facility was a branch of a larger facility elsewhere in the state.

They didn't believe the other facility could help either, given the severity of the allegations.

Facility Option 2: "No, we aren't equipped to deal with perpetrators of sexual assault. We primarily deal with adolescents who are engaged in self-harm or drug use. If she's suicidal, harming herself, or on drugs, we can help. Are you sure she isn't doing any of those things? Have you called option one?"

Yes, I started with option one and they couldn't help. Knowing what I've told you, you would agree to provide some sort of treatment if she were suicidal, self-harming, or on drugs, but because she hurt someone else, you can't help. Is there any place that can help disturbed adolescents who don't want to die or are on drugs? Moving on to option three.

Facility Option 3: "I'm sorry, we don't deal with perpetrators of sexual assault. Is she self-harming? Is she suicidal? Has she harmed animals? Because if she's harmed an animal, that shows predisposition to mental illness and we could intervene. Have you tried options one and two?

Okay, the first part of the conversation was old hat by this time, but the part about animals threw me for a loop. I laughed. I actually scoffed at the poor person on the phone who was just going through the list. You mean to tell me that if she had shoved an object up a cat's behind or choked an animal help would be available? I couldn't restrain myself. (If I had known of the sexual offenses to our pets, maybe we could have gotten somewhere. But alas, those details had not yet emerged.)

"Assaulting an animal shows predisposition for mental health problems, but sexually assaulting   another human being and attempting to take their life doesn't?!"

"Um, I'm sorry, Mam, but that's our policy. You see, unless she admits to what she has done, we   don't know that it actually happened. If you really feel that your younger daughter is potentially   in danger of future harm, or if you are fearful for her safety, you should take your oldest daughter to the emergency room for an evaluation or consider having your youngest child   admitted to our facility because she's been abused."

"Okay, first of all, my younger daughter, the victim, is not going anywhere. She needs her   parents, not a hospital. So you are saying that if we bring our oldest child to the emergency   room that we can get help?"

"Well, Mam, I can't make any promises, but we should be able to hold her temporarily in order   to keep your younger child safe. That will remove the danger from the home and give you time   to come up with an alternative plan for your older child or to move your younger child to a safe   place. Again, I can't guarantee that we will keep her. There is a chance that you will have to take   her back home with you."

Do I feel my youngest daughter is in danger? Yes. She fears for her very life. We have to do something.

So we took matters into our own hands, made the trip the emergency room with our oldest daughter and her admitted for five days to keep her little sister safe and figure out what to do. The nurses in the emergency room were amazing. However, once we were transferred to the adolescent unit and met the psychiatrist the following day, we were in for a rude awakening. We thought we were going to get help for our oldest child, little did we know that the psychiatrist we would encounter would be the defendant of the perpetrator. We quickly encountered a fast paced, unexpected, barrage of questions with an accusatory tone:

So, you actually think that she did this? I've spoken with her, and she says that she didn't do anything.

Why do you think she would lie?

You just found out? Are you sure you didn't know that this was going on the whole time?

Do you allow your children to view pornography?

I see in the family medical history that you suffered with Post-partum Depression (PPD) after you had your oldest child. What affect do you think this has had on her development and recent behaviors?

What is your highest degree of education?

Why would your younger daughter make these allegations?

She's just now coming forward with the information. Why do you think she waited so long to tell, IF it's true?

I read the written statement your youngest provided about the abuse. It was very graphic and used the appropriate terminology to describe what happened to her body. How do you think she came to know these words? This is all very serious. It's not our job to determine what has happened. Clearly, one of your daughter's is lying and needs a great deal of help.

These are just some of the questions and accusatory statements we were faced with that day. We answered them all and managed to keep our composure for the most part. Well, my husband kept his composure, but by the time we got to the final questions, I let this doctor know exactly how I felt about her attempts to vilify the victim. Again, I'm sure some of these questions are totally normal. In fact, they may be on a checklist somewhere. I simmered on this encounter and the response I wish I had given, but an accusatory tone was not at all what we had anticipated. We were left stunned and partially speechless, but if I could go back and do it over again, she would really get a piece of my mind.

So, you actually think that she did this? I've spoken with her, and she says that she didn't do anything. Why do you think she would lie?

Do I believe my oldest child has done this? Obviously. Do you think we are here for a vacation? Do you think this is our idea of fun? Do we think she would lie? YES! She has a history of being a perpetual liar and she's in trouble, of course she will lie to save her own skin.

You just found out? Are you sure you didn't know that this was going on the whole time? Do you allow your children to view pornography?

No, we had no idea this was happening. Had we known, it wouldn't have happened! Do we allow our children to watch pornography? Well, sure, we all sit down on the couch and watch it together like Saturday morning cartoons! You've got to be kidding me! Who does that?

One of the most damaging questions that haunted me for days concerned Post-Partum Depression. Mothers naturally tend to blame themselves when anything goes wrong. Somehow, the delayed bond between mother and child during those first few months had caused this. This is all my fault. As if the pain of enduring PPD wasn't difficult enough to endure at the time, you are telling me that my hormonal shift post-partum created a person capable of monstrous actions. I must be a bad mother. PPD caused me to be a bad mother from the beginning because we didn't bond instantly. All of the emotions and negative feelings I felt because I had PPD flooded to the surface and consumed my heart for days. Finally, I started to get my bearings emotionally.

I see in the family medical history that you suffered with Post-partum Depression (PPD) after you had your oldest child. What affect do you think this has had on her recent behaviors?

What impact do I think my PPD has had on her recent behaviors? None. Absolutely none. Nature vs nurture, I get it. I'm to blame because my nurturing was not on point at first. Please tell me how my depression during the first few months of this child's life caused her to exert her will to violently assault her sister sexually and attempt to take her life by strangulation 14-16 years later.

What is your highest degree of education?

What does our level of education have to do with our child's decisions to be violent? For the record, my husband holds a BA. I'm nearing completion of a PhD. Clearly by my educational level alone, I know how to research in-depth. I will not be told that I do not know anything about my child's mental health. In fact, let me tell you a thing or two, doc. I've gone through the DSM trying to figure out what is wrong with her for years. The counselors you supervise at this facility didn't want to listen. They weren't concerned about our parental worries. Their only concern was how the child felt. If someone had listened to me, you would know that she meets more than the minimum criteria for borderline personality disorder. But what do I know? I'm just a mom. Never mind that I've looked at the DSM IV and DSM 5 and spoken with another mental health professional. I know that borderline personality disorder can now be diagnosed as young as 16. However, you still won't diagnose her for a few reasons. It's a very serious thing to diagnose and you don't take that lightly. I get it, but can we go over the check list? Probably the real reason you won't even take it into consideration is that the DSM 5 hasn't gone into effect yet with insurance companies. They still operate on the definitions for diagnosis in the DSM IV. Yes, I've done my homework. I've read more about borderline personality disorder, diagnosis criteria, and treatments than the few I've encountered in the counseling profession. Anyone who dedicates their time and is willing to put forth the effort to learn can become knowledgeable. I know how to research. I'm good at it, and I don't get my information from Internet articles. Don't treat me like I'm ignorant. Go ahead, call me an educational snob, but I know criteria for the disorder and I know my oldest child. Use your level of education and help our daughter while there is still time.

Why would your younger daughter make these allegations? She's just now coming forward with the information. Why do you think she waited so long to tell, IF it's true?

Allegations – Why would my younger daughter not tell? Really? Her sister beat her, sexually assaulted her, and attempted to take her life by choking her until she nearly passed out. Hmmm...if someone was abusive, bigger, stronger, and kept me under thumb by intimidation, I would be AFRAID. Fear. Isn't that a good enough reason to not tell until now? Why do you think women who are abused often don't tell until they are adults? Some who are abused as a child don't tell until they are in their 50s, if ever! Thank God she told when she did, or she probably wouldn't have survived the next cycle of abuse.

I read the written statement your youngest provided about the abuse. It was very graphic and used the appropriate terminology to describe what happened to her body. How do you think she came to know these words?

Yes, my 14 year old knows the correct names for her body. Let's see, how could she know this information? Well, for starters, she's had a health class. We taught our children the proper names for anatomy when they were little. Boys have a penis, not a "p-bug" or a "wiener." Girls have a vagina, not a "coochie." Basically, she's 14, not 4. Wouldn't you find it strange if she didn't know these words at her age?

This is all very serious.

It's all very serious. Finally, we agree on something. Perhaps you see the need to help.

It's not our job to determine what has happened.

Okay, maybe it's not technically your job to determine what has happened. However, if CPS won't help and the police aren't going to investigate, then whose job is it?

Clearly, one of your daughter's is lying and needs a great deal of help.
Yes, obviously, one of our daughters is lying and needs a great deal of help. We have a clear track record of which child has continuously lied over the years. We've sought medical help and counseling services for her outrageous lying and concerning behaviors in the past. Some of them were right here in the department you oversee. Do you know what the testing resulted in? Inconclusive results because the patient "presented herself in an exceedingly positive light." Shouldn't that have raised concern right then, knowing the long, written parental report and notes taken by the counselor, per our discussion? Hey, why don't we look at some of the symptoms of borderline personality disorder? Guess what, exaggeration and viewing one's self in an exceedingly positive light is part of the package, along with many of her other symptoms that have been ongoing for years. Oh, but wait. We are just the parents. What would we know about these children, their predispositions, personalities, and behaviors? We've only been with them every day of their lives. Drop the accusatory tone and wipe that smug look off of your face. My youngest daughter has been diagnosed with PTSD by a doctor because of the trauma. She is currently unable to attend school and doesn't sleep because of night terrors. Pretend you are a professional and that you actually care about our family. That is part of your job, right?

The Friends & Family Dumb Shit

While our world was completely falling apart at the seams, one individual sent a bombardment of text messages wanting to know what we were going to tell our parents, co-workers, students, etc. We were facing, what was then, the worst day of our lives, yet it seemed this person was more concerned with appearances. I found myself comforting others about our situation. It didn't seem fair. Why weren't they trying to comfort us? I completely realize that those in our closest circle of friends and family were/are also affected by what happened. However, please realize that you are not the victim in this situation. Our oldest child is not the victim in this situation; she is the perpetrator. Our youngest daughter is the victim. Her safety and wellbeing are our first priority. After that, we have to deal with the needs of our other child, and finally, our own emotions. Pardon me if I don't have time, patience, or tolerance for your questions and to coddle your own emotional breakdown. Need to talk? Call our pastor; he knows what happened. Call HOPE, Inc. As a close family member, you have free counseling services there as a secondary victim. But for heaven's sake, keep your insensitive questions, comments, and unsolicited advice to yourself. It feels like I'm walking the center of a tightrope that's slowly burning from both ends. My children are on either side. I'm desperately trying to find a way to save both of them and make it to safety before time runs out. What happens if I can only reach one in time? I don't need anything else right now. Nonetheless, these are some of the real questions and statements made within the first 48 hours. Thankfully, exhaustion had set in and I didn't tell anyone what I really thought.

I'm trying to not fall apart and get through the day.

How nice. You are at work. Actually you are at my job, as a substitute, and I'm sitting in the hallway of the emergency room, waiting for my child to be admitted to the adolescent mental health ward. She refuses to speak to us or even make eye contact. My other child is with her godfather today. She's been diagnosed with PTSD. I've fallen apart more times in the last few days than you can imagine. My husband has been reduced to the rawest emotional state I've ever seen. We are a disaster! Do you want me to bring you a tissue? The nurses' station gave us an entire box for our tears. I'm sorry we told you. We thought you could handle it and be a support. By the way, why are you texting during class?

Is it nosey if I ask was it horrible today taking and leaving her there? Was there a scene? Can we visit? If so, when? Did they say how long they would keep her? I know that's a lot of questions, and maybe I shouldn't ask. Tell me if it is.

We hadn't even made it home from the hospital. My actual response was appropriate:

"Not now. It's been a long day, and it's not over. We are talked out."

Maybe you shouldn't ask? Trust me, you shouldn't. The course of our family has changed forever, and you want to know if it's horrible. Horrible isn't a strong enough word. I don't think you have any clue and have lost touch with reality by even asking this question. The rest of the questions, forget them. The first question left such a bitter taste in my mouth that you don't deserve any further response. Until your brain is working in conjunction with your mouth, stop talking. Not that it matters, but FYI, I changed clothes three times this morning. How stupid is that? But I couldn't even make a simple decision about what to wear because I felt like I was about to attend a funeral. I was attending a funeral; this was the official burial of our family unit as we knew it.

As our oldest daughter sat in acute care for five days, the comments continued to pour in from family. I know each individual has to process this in their own way. If you must talk to us about it, stop and consider the words that are about to shoot from your mouth like a fiery arrow and lodge in our hearts and minds.

It's just normal teen hormones. It's just sin nature.

Stop downplaying what has happened. If you include the word "just" in your statement, you are attempting to minimize the damage and make excuses for the perpetrator. Are teenagers hormonal? Of course. Does mankind have the potential for evil? Yes. However, an individual of average intelligence who knows right from wrong is not absolved from bad behavior because of hormones or the natural inclination to do wrong if accountability can be potentially avoided. There is nothing normal about raping someone. There is nothing normal about violence. There is nothing normal about attempting murder. You don't know what has really happened. We're trying to save you from the horrible details. Just know that we are doing the best we can for both of our children.

I feel like I've lost my family.

Really? Go ahead and tell me about how you feel like you've lost your family. Yes, you are a member of the family, but they are OUR DAUGHTERS! Our family will never be the same. We feel that we have lost both of our children to an extent. First, our baby has had her innocence violently ripped from her. Her self-esteem has been shattered. It's a miracle she's still alive. It will take a long time to rebuild her into the young woman she is destined to be, one who knows her value and won't live the life of a victim. Secondly, our oldest daughter is currently in acute care. We don't know if she will face the court system and go to juvenile detention or if she will have to be in residential care for a while. All we know is that she will not be able to live at home for quite some time, if ever. We have lost our family. Our family unit is broken. It has been broken for two years, and we just found out precisely how messed up things have been. We pray for restoration, but that will take a lot of professional help, time, and divine intervention. Please, keep these feelings to yourself. I don't have the strength to comfort you and survive at the same time.

I know this is probably hard on you all too.

Just look at this statement. This is probably hard on you too. Probably? Hard? Too? (As if we are somehow lower members on the totem pole that has fallen into the abyss.) *No. Neither do you have any idea what this is "probably" like, nor do you know the definition of "hard." Please, be quiet before I say something I should "probably" regret but won't.*

The dumb shit didn't stop in the weeks and months ahead.

Remember, you have two daughters in this.

This statement and others like it were uttered by more than one family member at various times in the journey and by far is one of the most painful.

Yes, we are very aware that we have two daughters in this. This is the worst situation we could find ourselves in. Do you think we take this lightly? Do you think this is easy? Just because we are able to take swift action and refuse to sweep this under the rug and pretend it didn't happen doesn't mean we don't care about the oldest child. In fact, it means we care a whole lot more than anyone else does because we are doing what's in the best interest of BOTH children. A little support and understanding would go a long way right now, while we rattle every cage in hell to keep our youngest child safe and get help for our oldest. Would YOU please remember that we have two daughters in this? Because the only person you seem concerned about is the perpetrator. Remember, you don't know all the details. You have made it clear that you don't want to know the details of the abuse. Please respect us as we make decisions that are more difficult than you can comprehend. Even if you don't agree, show some respect.

(Speaking of our oldest in acute care while looking for residential treatment…) You know she may hate you forever for this.

Thank you for being a ray of sunshine and pointing out the positive. She's hated us for years for taking her to counseling. She's hated us because she hasn't gotten away with incessant lying. She's hated us for her not being the center of the universe, so I guess hatred won't be anything new. Of course we know she may hate us forever for not believing her lies and forcing her to get help outside of the home. Would you rather she stay in the home and continue to rape, beat, and attempt to murder her sister? Would it be better if our youngest child were permanently damaged from being cast aside in disbelief and have her hate us forever for not protecting her? Would it be better if we cared more for the perpetrator's feelings and allowed her to murder her sister or cause brain damage that would leave her in a vegetative state just so she won't hate us? Get some perspective. The perpetrator is not the victim.

She could just stay with us. (500 feet away)

What a great idea! Let's allow the perpetrator to live next door. The victim can forever live in fear and be a prisoner in her own home. Excellent solution. Problem solved. Nothing could go wrong with this plan.

It's a good thing she isn't a boy!

Did your brain actually process those words before they came out of your mouth? Guess what, girls can be rapists too. Our oldest child is one of them. Just because she doesn't have male anatomy doesn't mean that she didn't commit the same act. Do you think that having multiple objects forcefully shoved into the vagina isn't rape? Some of those objects were larger than an actual penis. Perhaps you mean we are lucky because there is no chance of pregnancy? I really don't know what you mean by this, but stop talking. Your ignorance is blazing through the night sky like fireworks on the 4th of July.

Chapter 8: The Next Phase

After five days of residential care, our oldest was discharged. She moved in with her godparent and began counseling at a crisis center an hour from home. My husband would meet them after working midnight shift and take her to the counseling center, while her godparent went to work. She remained in this program for 15 days.

I took our youngest daughter to weekly counseling and she completed a forensic interview, recounting the graphic details of the abuse to a total stranger, while live streaming to the crimes against children officer in the other room. It was one of the most difficult moments of the journey to that point. I was embarrassed because the officer was from my home town, he knew my parents, and I had his family members as students. He's a professional, but would he judge us behind closed doors? Not that it's important in the whole scheme of things, but the embarrassment and shame associated with this type of abuse is what keeps people silent. I knew we were doing the right thing, but would our tiny, small-town world soon know the details of our nightmare? How would that impact our kids?

The thought of having to relive the details of the abuse and answer intimate questions posed by a stranger made our daughter physically sick. I tried my best to reassure her and encouraged her to be brave and answer everything honestly with as much detail as she could. As we sat in the parking lot waiting to go in, she looked so tiny and afraid. It was if she was a toddler again and I wanted desperately to hold her in my lap and make it all disappear like a bad dream. After the interview was complete, the officer met with me privately. He was professional, yet clearly exhibited sympathy. Thankfully, I didn't sense an ounce of judgement as he expressed that this type of thing happens in all walks of life. This didn't mean that we were bad parents. In fact, after speaking with our daughter, he thought we were good parents who wanted to believe the best of our children and didn't see the warning signs, as most people don't. He explained that in over 20 years in this field, he was certain that the abuse occurred and that based on the interview, he didn't question the validity of any of the accusations. We must keep our children apart at all costs. A separate interview with the perpetrator would be conducted. He couldn't tell me what the outcome would be. I expressed that we didn't want to press charges against our oldest child and forever mark her future; we wanted to get her professional help and rehabilitation. (We may never know if this was the right decision.) With that knowledge and our current efforts to locate a residential facility that specialized in female sexual abusers, he concluded our talk by speaking with the victim, reassuring her that she hadn't done anything wrong, explaining that what happened to her was a crime, and that he would do everything in his power to make sure she was safe. Her sister would not return home. Meanwhile, more "support" and advice kept coming in. It provided as much comfort as a leaky roof in the middle of a torrential downpour.

Chapter 9: And the Dumb Shit Goes On

Remember, she's your daughter too.

Yes, we've been over this sentiment before. Now we've heard it from both sets of parents. Do you really think we've forgotten? We are quite aware of the needs of both children. We are doing all we can to help each of them. Yes, I'm the one who is trying to support the victim and take her to all of her appointments, while my husband takes care of our oldest daughter's needs. We are not super human. It's impossible to be two places at the same time. It's impossible to time travel and circumvent the demands of driving. I haven't forgotten my oldest daughter, but I do have another child who needs care and a parent at all times. We are really doing the best we can for each child and right now that means we must divide and conquer the tasks ahead.

How do you choose one child over the other?

How is taking care of both children choosing one over the other? If both of my children had been in a car accident and needed different kinds of physical care and/or therapy and my husband and I took them to their respective appointments based on proximity of our workplace, would I be choosing one over the other? Somehow, I think you would believe we were doing the best we could, given the situation. This is no different. We are not choosing sides. We are running the roads to get the care each child needs. Do I believe one child over the other? Yes. If you knew what I know, you would believe too. Am I justified in my ability to know who to believe? Yes. You haven't lived in our home to know what we've dealt with for years. If believing the abused over the abuser is choosing a side, then I choose truth over lies, I choose protection and safety over continual subjection to horror and possibly death, and I choose making the hard decisions that you cannot comprehend. I choose life, hope, and future wholeness in my decision to not look away and pretend this didn't happen. Would you make these choices? Based on many conversations where you have unintentionally blamed the victim and insinuated that you would not have removed the perpetrator from the home, you would not. Your refusal to look at the horrifying reality of what has happened would result in the death of my youngest child, physically by the hand of her sister or possibly by ending her own life to stop the abuse, or mentally and emotionally from refusing to help when the truth was revealed. I will continue to choose truth, life, and hope for wholeness, regardless of your opinion.

Speaking of the victim,

I couldn't deal with the PTSD/anxiety stuff. In my day, we just moved on. You need to make her go back to school.

Thank you for your lack of concern for the victim and failure to realize that she has been severely traumatized. Yes, in your day you might have "just moved on." But the effects of abuse that aren't dealt with will cause further damage for years. I know you don't understand, but know that we are doing what is best for her mental and emotional well-being. She isn't going to school right now because she has no focus, the triggers of PTSD are continually emerging. She can't handle the stress and needs time to recover.

She's just going to have to get over it. I know what it's like to have PTSD, and she just has to get over it.

I really wish it was that simple. It would be awesome if there was a "get over it button" and we could fast forward through this section of recovery and find wholeness. There isn't. This is a process. I know you know what it's like to have PTSD. Yes, you have dealt with it personally; however, no two experiences are alike. Your PTSD was not caused by sexual trauma, neither was it perpetrated by a family member; you are a veteran. While I am grateful for your service to our country, the cause of the trauma significantly changes the nature of the situation. In addition, how many years has it been since you were in the military? Yet you have had to address the issues of PTSD many years after the fact. You should know that this impacts the life of the sufferer in many ways that others do not comprehend. Please consider your age when you were traumatized. You were a young adult, not a 12-14 year old whose ability to reason isn't fully developed at this time.

She can recover if given the proper care, time, and respect. Just because she is a child doesn't diminish her struggle. Please be sensitive to the triggers we know. Don't say insensitive things like, "What's wrong with you!?" Don't be offended or cold when she can't handle triggers and chooses to remove herself from the situation. She is vulnerable and needs your understanding more than you realize. There are a lot of things that are wrong right now. Sometimes we wonder if things will ever feel right again, but we pray they will. Denial and repression do not equate "getting over it," and it is in her best interest to work through the trauma at her own pace so that it doesn't affect every aspect of her life for years to come. Maybe it's time to offer some compassion and get over the idea of just getting over it.

You are strong. That's why God chose you to go through this. You are being tested, but you will be okay.

I understand the concept behind these types of statements. People are well meaning and say things that they think are comforting because they don't know what else to say. I know this individual meant no harm. After all, how many times has someone said something similar after the death of a loved one? You know, insensitive statements such as, "They are better off now." or "God must have needed another angel." Just as those hollow statements hold no balm for one who is grieving, neither does attempting to somehow make this part of the divine plan.

I refuse to believe that God chose my youngest child to be brutally raped and abused. I refuse to believe that God chose my oldest child to possibly have a personality disorder. I refuse to believe that it was in the divine plan for her to sexually assault and attempt to kill her sister. I don't believe God predestined our family to go through this. Would you tell a parent of a child with terminal cancer that God chose them to suffer for years? Would you tell the survivors of any tragic loss that God chose them? I know this is not a malicious statement, but God didn't choose these actions. My oldest daughter is responsible for her decisions, not God.

Because of the actions of our oldest child, we are being tested to the breaking point in every possible way. Our family unit is being tested. Our relationship with each of our children is being tested. Our marriage is being tested. Our relationship with our parents is being tested. Our relationships with other family members and friends are being tested. Our ability to work, manage finances, think, and simply live is being tested. Our faith is being tested. Are we strong? No. We are anything but strong. However, we have no choice but to put one foot in front of the other. We know where our strength lies, and with God's help and maintaining our relationship as a couple, this family will survive. Will our children ever have a restored relationship? I don't know. Right now that isn't what's important. Safety, protection, healing, personal restoration, and providing hope is the focus. Will our relationships with others remain the same? Time will tell. I'm sure some will weaken while others grow stronger. Few are able to walk this road with us and provide true love, friendship, and support. Will we look the same on the other side? No. We will have battle scars that carry enough love, sweat, and tears to represent a battalion. Will we be okay? That depends on your definition. We will never be the same. We are forever changed, but our hope as parents in the midst of the devastation is that we will each emerge healthy. While God did not predestine this to happen, we believe that we will rise from the ashes and be able to help others because of our experience. Right now, this seems like a lofty goal, but we have faith and each other. We will survive.

I just don't see why it has to be this way!

This comment, along with similar sentiments often came from family members. Some knew the depths of the abuse, while other sat in judgement from the peanut gallery. First of all, if you don't know the facts, I guess you are justified in your thought process; however, look more closely at the surface information that you can gather and I'm sure you can put two and two together and come up with four. It's pretty simple. Our oldest child is living with a family friend after spending four months in residential care, you know she was violent toward her sister and a danger to the home. Our youngest is in therapy and now has a service dog. Let's see....I would think that basic logic would say that our oldest did something horrifying and that we are doing our best to care for both of them while ensuring safety. Make sense?

To those who know the truth, this statement further displays your lack of concern for the sanctity of life and your desire to sweep what happened aside. You know exactly why it has to be this way and agree, except for when you want to forget and have things return to "normal." News flash number one, things were not normal before and we will never meet your definition of normal in the future. News flash number two, it's not about you and your feelings. Furthermore, the fact that this concept is recurring makes us wish that we were able to pack our bags and completely relocate.

Not only were stupid and insensitive statements made to us, but our youngest child had to endure her own amount of dumb shit. Some of the statements made toward her came from students at school and others from "well intentioned" family members. By far, the most frequent sentiments she received was that she should just suck it up and get over it or that she didn't really need a service dog. One boy was mean enough to tell her that nobody would ever want her now because of what happened to her. Unfortunately, I can't fight her battles for her. I certainly wanted to give each individual who made her feel inferior a piece of my mind. Obviously, she can't just suck it up and move on. If the doctors and judge hadn't felt she needed a service dog, the financial award would not have been granted. She doesn't "just" have anxiety. PTSD is a completely different condition. Regardless of your age, please educate yourself before giving your opinion. Better yet, keep your opinion to yourself and don't make insensitive statements to my child. You have no idea what she has been through.

Chapter 10: Friends of Faith

Christian friends try to do all they can to provide comfort. Sharing the same faith base does provide common ground, and as a person of faith, I understand and appreciate the sentiment. However, sometimes timing is everything. Yes, God will get us through this. Yes, I still believe Jeremiah 29:11 that God has a plan for us, but sometimes the best thing you can do is to just be supportive with your presence. Do something simple like send a text message or a card. Better yet, do something practical. A short sermon, reminders of spiritual truths, or lengthy prayers are not always what is needed at the moment. None the less, friends of faith unintentionally added to the crap load.

In times like these, you just have to worship. I'm going to pray for you about this, and then you are going to pray for me because you have to pick yourself back up. (The friend then proceeds praying, quoting from Psalms, and telling the story of David.)

I don't like admitting that I need help, but I was in full meltdown mode while driving down the Interstate alone. I decided to reach out. I was a little bit shocked by the reminder that I just needed to worship. Yes, it's true. God can really minister to us through worship and it is a reminder of His faithfulness. Yes, I need to be reminded of these things. But right now, I need to just be human.

Can I please stop trying to keep it together for just a few minutes and cry with a support person? I need someone to listen. I need to be permitted to let out some of these emotions and to vent with someone else who isn't in the depths of hell alongside me. I know you can't fix it. I don't expect you to fix it. I don't even expect you to have any profound words of wisdom. I know that this situation is outside the norm for everyone and no one knows what to do or how to support us right now. As my friend, you are shocked too. Please just let me be real. I spend the majority of my time putting on a mask to the world, attempting to look like I've still got it together in order to survive daily tasks like buying a gallon of milk and a loaf of bread or putting fuel in my car without spontaneously turning into a puddle of tears.

You're going to pray for me. Great. Maybe God can use your words to push back the darkness a little or comfort my racing thoughts, but I don't need to pray for you. Sorry. I know that sometimes in our greatest need and during our times of lack that giving back to others can take the focus off our circumstances and redirect things in a positive direction. Today is not that day. I'm spiritually bankrupt. I am truly not capable of forming thoughts into a prayer, other than to simply say "Jesus." That's all I've got left. When I've found any words to send toward heaven, they have been filled with "I don't know what to do! How could this happen? Is there any hope for us? WHY!?" But those aren't prayers, those are one sided ranting sessions.

As I continued driving down the Interstate with my friend praying a million miles a minute and telling the story of David, I completely disconnected. I went from what was a real, raw moment in need of support, to being completely turned off by the very thing that should have provided comfort. I was numb. I was somewhat angry as I considered the fact that when he stopped praying he wanted me to pray for him to help pick myself back up. This was not one of my finer moments. I like to be strong. Melting down and allowing myself to be vulnerable is a rarity, and the response I received is not what I expected or needed at the moment.

Sometimes talking on a cell phone is a true blessing. As he continued to pray for several more minutes, in my disconnected state I couldn't take it anymore. I did one of the most embarrassing things I can admit to doing to a friend who was genuinely trying to help. I turned down the volume in my car so I couldn't hear him, drove about a mile, and hung up. Yes, it's horrible. Yes, I'm still slightly ashamed of my inability and unwillingness to be more direct, which is generally my personality. But I couldn't do it. I couldn't pick myself up. I couldn't tell him to just stop and listen to me. I couldn't do anything but shut down and cry myself the remaining 20 miles until I had to see someone face to face.

I know what your youngest is going through because my cousin/friend/whoever has PTSD. I've read some about it; probably not as much as you have. But the person I know went through far worse than your daughter. Your daughter just needs to really press into God and allow Him to take care of this.

Where do I begin? You know what my child feels like because you have knowledge based on the experience of another person. Sure, that's a great understanding of PTSD. Thank you for taking the time to read and become informed about the condition; however, you might need to take the time to read more so you don't make insensitive comments like this. I'm sorry someone you were close to endured the horror of sexual trauma and abuse, but do not compare one experience to the other. I'm glad she was able to find comfort in her faith and move forward. Right now, our daughter's faith is shaken. She watched her sister live a double life, one of spirituality and the other of a monster. Her friends from church and youth pastor don't know how to respond, so they do nothing for fear of doing the wrong thing. She is unable to fully comprehend their perspective and only feels abandoned and rejected by the church world. She feels abandoned by God. How could He let this happen to her? Those are totally normal thoughts and feelings. Has she totally abandoned her faith? No. She often says that when she gets through this she will have an amazing testimony and be able to help others. But guess what? She's 15; she isn't there yet, and that's okay. Please, never assume you know what someone is going through, compare tragedy, or suggest that anyone just needs a little more spirituality and all will be well.

Another common trend from my friends of faith was the offer to listen. Many offered to listen, but few understood the concept. When offering to listen, please do that. Don't interrupt. If I become emotional, please let me be human. I know it's uncomfortable to support someone who is crying, but if you find me in that state, please let me be real. I know I'm generally the strong one, but I'm not always strong. And please, don't tell me that you know how I feel. You don't. You really don't. The fact that your mother is bipolar, your cousin has PTSD, or your great-grandma twice removed had an undiagnosed personality disorder is very unfortunate and I sympathize, but it doesn't mean you know how I feel. Several people offered comparisons to another family member's mental health struggle or to issues with a rebellious child, but we are dealing with a multi-faceted issue involving both of our children. Your comparisons are not helpful. You offered to listen, remember?

You need to be putting the Word in her every day. We all need daily, spiritual food, just like we need regular food. You need to make time to sit down with her every day and do a devotion. You just need to keep putting the Word in her and speaking the Word over her every day.

Okay, call me a bad Christian. Do I believe the Bible? Yes. But right now, slapping a "Jesus sticker" on it or beating us with the Bible isn't going to help anyone. Our faith has been shaken to the core. Our daughter is questioning her faith in many aspects, and at times has asked the age old question, "Why did God let this happen?" Beating her over the head with a devotional is not what she needs at the moment. In fact, I believe it would do more harm than good. It would probably turn her away from faith in disgust, just like watching her sister's spiritual hypocrisy was and remains nauseating.

Here is the truth, friend of faith who believes daily devotions to be the answer. Each member of our family is on this journey. We are in different places spiritually, mentally, and emotionally. We are in different phases of the grieving process, and we have much to grieve individually and as a family unit. Sometimes we each question God. We have each been angry with God. We each still believe in God, but our faith in what God will do in this situation varies. My husband reads his Bible daily and does all of the things that Christianity prescribes in crisis. I'm glad he does those things. He finds comfort and peace in those things. My devotional time isn't as consistent as his; however, my spiritual walk isn't compromised. Our youngest daughter still believes, but she feels betrayed spiritually. You see, the church turned a blind eye to her. She has been the invisible victim. This situation was beyond the capabilities of her youth pastor who has had little to no contact. Her Christian friends faded away. One even sent a text to express that she needed to distance herself from their friendship because she didn't know how to help.

In spite of all of this, the fact remains that God knows exactly where we are individually, and He's okay with that! Only the Divine is capable of understanding our grief, sorrow, anger, and host of other emotions. Most importantly, God knows how to reach us on a personal level. Only the one who created the human heart knows exactly how to whisper or provide gentle reminders that we aren't forgotten on this journey. Daily devotionals might be the answer for some, but please remember that there is not a one size fits all approach.

Chapter 11: The Transition

Toward the end of the 15 days of crisis counseling, the psychiatric/counseling team met and discussed the situation to determine what motivated our oldest daughter. They determined that she loved two things above all else, herself and control. After meeting with us for a family session, seeing the complete void of emotion as she read a few entries from a journal, further questions, and a separate discussion with us, they determined, without reservation, that she was lying. The following day they discussed the allegations and potential consequences with her again, and she confessed to almost everything. She admitted to being insanely jealous of her sister, having feelings of hatred, demonstrating sexually inappropriate behavior, and brutality. "Don't you think I hate myself for what I've done?!" she shouted at her father. A breakthrough! We thought this would be the beginning of the healing process. However, after the confession, she shut down completely with her counselor. With no further progress and refusal to discuss the issues, the crisis counseling was complete. Do I believe she hates herself for what she's done? I'm not certain. I believe she is angry she got caught. She exhibits no sign of remorse for her actions, the pain caused to her sister or our family, or concern for how her sister is doing. If she really felt remorse for what she has done, wouldn't she respond differently?

In order to provide stability and continue regular outpatient counseling, she moved to her grandparents' house. As retirees, this would remove the concern of supervision during the day. There, she would participate in weekly outpatient counseling and await an interview with the state police. Again, I was faced with personal embarrassment and feelings of shame as the name of the counselor was revealed. He was a former student. Great. Now someone else in my tiny home town will know all of our business. He met with me privately to gather the big picture and discuss the notes that had been shared from the previous counselor, his superior. He encouraged me to take time for myself and that we all should seek individual counseling. While I'm sure this is a wonderful idea and we would have benefited, there simply wasn't a spare moment to seek personal care. We were in pure survival mode and doing well just to put one foot in front of the other.

He was determined to figure out what caused her behavior. I discussed the possibility of borderline personality disorder and family history that seemed to be present in previous generations, although it was undiagnosed. Even though he appeared to listen, my concerns and explanation of family history seemed dismissed. I should have known he would fall victim to her manipulative stories when he expressed, "We have to find the hurt caused to little "Brittney." She's a victim too. Hurt people hurt people." If we had been abusive or neglectful parents, I could understand this reasoning. Once again it seemed that her choices had to have a simple root in having been abused or improper parental care along the way.

It seems that few mental health professionals are willing to look at genetic predisposition and family history of mental illness. We talked for hours, recounting all the oddities I could remember over the years and things, which in hindsight, were clearly warning signs. He took notes. I tried to feel hopeful. When we concluded, he asked me what my personal feelings were about the situation. I told him I was angry. I was angry at myself for not seeing the warning signs sooner. I was angry at all the professionals who refused to listen to this ranting mother when I tried to explain that there was some deeply rooted problem with my child and she was capable of harming someone. I was angry with the perpetrator. How could she do this to her sister? In what alter universe did she believe that it was acceptable to exert her will over another human being, inflict pain, attempt to take a life, manipulate, lie, and cause someone to live in fear? I was angry that the system had failed us. At times, I was angry at God. As we exited the building and stood on the stoop with the rain pouring inches in front of us, he responded and identified himself as a person of faith.

"You can choose to not be angry. Just like you choose to forgive, you can decide this moment to no longer experience anger."

Now isn't that a nice little answer? In that moment, I was relieved that the pouring rain resounded a roar in the parking lot that matched the roar in my brain. I felt like a less than Christian. Clearly, I could choose to forgive. According to this counselor, I could choose right now, this very moment, to not be angry at my daughter for raping her sister and attempting to choke her to death. Feeling belittled and betrayed by my own emotions, I ran through the rain to my car and cried again for all things lost and my inability to exert my will over my emotions in order to no longer experience anger. Apparently, I just needed to have more faith. I needed to be more like Jesus and forgive. I choose to forgive, but that does not mean I forget. I should not forget. My youngest child will never forget. Since then, I have learned that anger is not necessarily a negative emotion and that forgiveness isn't always so simple. I have a right to be angry that injustice was done. Anger is an appropriate emotion.

We were working toward residential care and were waiting for all agencies to complete protocol and give approval. This counselor was just a step along the path to where we needed to be, and I understood that. He, however, did not. Bless his heart, he actually thought he could help her. After meeting with her for about three weeks, for approximately an hour each week, our daughter told her grandmother that the counselor did not think she needed residential care because he could help her with her problems. My mother hadn't been impressed with the temperament of the counselor all along. Yes, a certain amount of joking is useful in breaking the ice and making the client more comfortable, but my mother found his ongoing tomfoolery inappropriate for the situation. At one point he addressed my mother in the waiting room saying, "You look so serious." Her response was priceless, "I think this is a very serious situation, don't you?" Unsure if the reports of his belief that she did not need residential care, I contacted him. Much to my surprise, my daughter hadn't completely lied about the situation and the professional dumb shit continued.

I do think I can help her. Why do you think she needs residential care? Why that facility? She says she doesn't want to go. I just want what's in the best interest of your child. I'm thinking of your entire family.

At this point in the journey, I had lost a large portion of my filter. I had dealt with enough insensitive comments. I was tired of defending our decisions and wouldn't tolerate any more insinuations that we did not want what was in the best interest of both of our children.

"First of all, what she wants isn't important. What she needs is. Just like an addict doesn't want rehabilitation, their addiction will destroy everyone around them, and then they self-destruct."

"But some addicts need different types of treatment. My goal is reconciliation and forgiveness for all of you."

"I'm glad you think you can help, but this is out of your league. This requires specialized care. Reconciliation and forgiveness can only happen after she gets help. Hopefully, the professionals at the facility will be willing to see the mental health issue underneath."

"I see the mental health issues underneath too. "

"If you see the possibility of a mental health issue, possibly a personality disorder, then you know she needs intensive, residential care."

"That's what troubles me."

"After doing my homework, speaking with a mental health professional who is ABD in mental health counseling, and taking the advice of the crisis center, it seems that it's the best option for successful treatment. Is it tough? Yes. Is it necessary? Yes. I'm sorry if you think I'm brutal, but I've been dealing with her problems a long time. I feared she would eventually harm someone. I've educated myself as well as I can. I've read more about personality disorders, specifically BPD, than some in the field. I'm sure you're a great counselor, but this requires more than you can provide. Any indication that she can be helped here and that it isn't serious enough to need residential care feeds her delusion about the situation and the lies she tells herself."

"So it's like I gave her another argument to throw at you."

"Yes. I know it wasn't your intention, but she uses anything against us she can grab hold of, twist, or fabricate."

In fact, she went so far as to tell my mother that she thought the counselor at the crisis center must have mixed up another client's file with hers because she didn't admit to anything. She didn't confess anything. She didn't say any of the things that were in her file. There must be a mistake.

Later, the story deviated again and the counselor at the crisis center had baited her with leading questions, misinterpreted her answers when she said it had all been consensual, and then wrote down what she wanted. She didn't do anything wrong. Her sister was lying, and everyone, including the counselor at the crisis center, was against her.

Chapter 12: Entering Residential Treatment

After about 20 days, things were moving forward with residential care. We received the remaining paperwork that would need to be completed at admission and the dress code that required a shopping spree. Within a week, we received the phone call we had been waiting for. Everything was approved. The insurance would cover costs after the initial co-pay. We had 24 hours to get her things together and make our way to Tennessee. We knew this day was coming. We just didn't know it would be so soon. It was both a relief and a heartbreak. This was it. This was real. We were about to take our oldest child eight hours away and leave her in a strange place for an undetermined amount of time. Will the insurance continue to approve after three months? Statistically, she needs a minimum of six to nine months to make any progress. Will she be there until she's 18? What then? She will never be able to live under our roof again. Depending on how long she's there, will she be able to obtain the credits needed to graduate high school? Will she need to get her GED? So many questions with so few answers. Conflicting emotions ruled the day. We made arrangements for our youngest to be cared for and made the long journey with a child who hated us for what we were doing to her. She was unable to see that her actions dictated our choices and she was lucky the legal system initially dropped the ball and later decided that rehabilitation is preferable to juvenile detention.

We arrived at the facility. Of course, it's gated. We couldn't help but feel as if we were approaching a prison at the front gate, armed with a camera and guard. We were flustered as we parked the car. My husband reminded her that we were doing this because we loved her and wanted our family back. She was silent, as she had been for many miles. The campus was comprised of attractive brick buildings and had a pretty courtyard. We entered, gave our names, brought her personal items in for check-in, and played checkers on a large table while we anxiously awaited whatever would happen next. We were greeted by the admissions counselor and intake nurses and taken through several locked doors to the general exam room where they took her vitals and we completed paperwork. It was a streamlined process. Before we knew it, it was time to go.

"You might want to give your mom and dad a hug now, because it's time for them to go."

It reminded me of when you leave your child at school for the first time or drop them off at summer camp. You walk away worried, anxious, and feeling empty. You know they will be okay, but it doesn't change the awkward process of leaving for the first time and the void that follows the heart of the parent. She reluctantly gave us a hug and we made our way out of the locked door to the waiting area. The receptionist gave us a knowing glance and nod, understanding that we had just done the most difficult thing we had ever had to do as parents. As we opened the front door and stepped onto the porch, our eyes burned with tears. My husband cried all the way to the car. Were we doing the right thing? We knew we were, but it was heartbreaking. We sat in the parking lot and cried together. When we tried to leave, we didn't have a firm plan of what we would do. As we drove, I had a horrible panic attack. My husband was relying on me to use my phone to locate a hotel and give directions, but my brain shut down. I didn't know how to use my phone. I couldn't think. I could hardly breathe. He decided to drive through a residential area until we stopped in a parking lot and sobbed some more. Finally, we were able to compose ourselves a little, regain brain function, and locate a hotel and dinner. All of our actions were mechanical.

She called several times that night. She was scared. She wanted to go home. She didn't have her personal belongings yet, and it was past the time they said she would receive them. We questioned our decision. Was this really the right place? It was recommended and sported a positive success rate, but why weren't they taking care of her? We could hear girls arguing in the background on the unit. Was she safe? Should we go get her? Wasn't there another way to get her the help she desperately needed? We started making phone calls and dialing the extensions provided to obtain answers regarding her things, her fears, and the chaos in the background. We couldn't get through at first. We kept calling. When we did get through to the unit, it was explained that there had been a problem between some of the girls that had taken their attention, causing the delay in her personal belongings getting checked in properly, but she would have them soon. We were reminded that this is a mental health facility and sometimes there are issues with the clients, but that safety was the number one priority. We spoke with her the next morning before we started the long drive home. Things had settled down. She was very unhappy, but she was safe.

For a few days, most of the extended family was subdued. She was gone. They were permitted to write. She could make two phone calls two days a week and an additional phone call on Sunday, if unit behavior and time permitted. We dealt with our own emotions and resumed the care of our only child at home whose emotional needs were great. I made her wellbeing my focus. I had done all I could do to help my oldest child; she was in the only place we could access to possibly help her. In order to cope, maintain my sanity, and provide proper care for our youngest, I had to detach from the negative emotions associated with leaving our daughter in a residential facility. This doesn't mean that I cared any less, but I couldn't remain in mourning over my child getting the care she needed, care for my other daughter, work, and maintain my own physical and mental health. My ability to do this created tension with my mother who misinterpreted my lack of continual mourning over her absence as a lack of love. One week after admission to the residential facility, she addressed her concern.

"You know, it really bothers me that you are able to distance yourself from this to make those decisions. It's like you only focus on what's best for one child. You can't harden your heart against your daughter; that's un-forgiveness. It's as if you have one child, while your husband still has two."

I don't remember what I said that day. I know I tried to defend our decisions. I explained the situation again and tried to remain respectful, but the impact of this statement was one of the most difficult to overcome. I was accused, by my own mother, of being a bad parent. My husband was the good parent.

I'm sorry that you don't understand my ability to distance myself from the raw emotions and make difficult decisions. Maybe that makes me heartless. Many say it makes me strong and a good mother. I'm not just focusing on one child. Trust me, I'm focusing on both intensely, but you can't see that because you are only focused on the oldest. You have yet to comprehend the destruction to my youngest child. Demonstrating tough love doesn't mean that my heart is hardened. Rather, the total opposite is true. Have I forgiven my daughter for assaulting and attempting to take the life of my other child? Not completely, not yet. I'm sure I'll get there in time, but I know you, Mom. If someone had done these acts to me, you wouldn't be quick to forgive. You would want justice. I can't have justice because both are my children, so I have to pray for rehabilitation for the perpetrator and healing for the victim. Justice will never be served. Grace, mercy, and unconditional love have been demonstrated. I'm sorry you think I behave as if I only have one child and my husband is the better parent, but I'm the one on the frontline confronting the nightmares, panic attacks, and demons my youngest child faces 24/7 as one with PTSD. I'm sorry you can't understand the implications that this diagnosis has on her life and on ours. I have two children. My heart is divided, but I have one child in front of me every day who needs me more than I need to breathe. Yes, I will devote every fiber of my being to her recovery. If this had happened to me, as my mother, I hope you would have done the same. I hope one day you can see me as my husband sees me, a mother who loves fiercely and will shake hell to save her children.

Over time, the sting of this statement lessened and our relationship returned to normal.

By this time, everyone treated us differently. We saw the sad looks, awkward glances, and friendly avoidance of those who were acquaintances and many who we thought were friends but were uncomfortable with the situation. However, that Sunday, a friend approached us at church. With eyes filled with concern he asked,

"How are you guys doing?"

My husband buffered this one. I wasn't in any mood for questions and was ready to fall apart if I made direct eye contact with anyone.

"Okay."

"Just okay?"

"Well, you can't ask for much better right now."

He tried to be encouraging by reminding us that God would be faithful and that things would get better in time. I couldn't help but roll my eyes to myself and wonder what else we should be and why "okay" wasn't an acceptable condition. What should we be? Spectacular? Thrilled that our family is in shambles? Excited that one child is out of state in residential care and the other is struggling to function every day because of PTSD? Fortunate because we are suffering and we should count it all joy? Sorry, we're struggling today. We're emotionally, mentally, spiritually, and physically exhausted. I think "okay" is a perfectly acceptable condition, all things considered.

Our insurance case manager, who has a counseling degree, warned us that it could take two to three months before our oldest daughter would confess. It's a normal part of the process. We didn't expect much for the first couple of months. The counselor who was assigned her case met with us personally and listened intently to the entire 17 years of concerning behaviors. At the conclusion of our discussion, she also mentioned the possibility of a personality disorder; however, that would be up to the psychiatrists. Within a few weeks, I was contacted by two psychiatrists at the facility who thought a personality disorder might be the central issue. Maybe a diagnosis would be possible after all. A diagnosis would lead to a better treatment plan and rehabilitation. They should have told us up front that they would not diagnose a personality disorder under the age of 18. We would have found a facility better equipped to make that determination. Instead, our time and resources were wasted during her stay in residential care. Because of their unwillingness or inability to diagnose what they believed to be true, she may never have a diagnosis and receive the treatment she needs.

After a month of counseling and our daughter's refusal to participate in family counseling sessions, which were a requirement of the treatment plan, the counselor suggested the case be handed to someone else.

"I just don't think I can reach her. My primary job is to deal with victims."

We appreciated the honesty, but why did it take a month to realize that someone who primarily deals with victims might not be the proper fit?

The case was handed to a new counselor who described herself as very assertive, straight-forward, and keeping close tabs on her clients. The first family session wasn't what we expected. She had been there over a month, but we found ourselves going over the history and entire story again. Okay, maybe this was necessary, but everything was in the file. Can we please move on to where things are now? This counselor made it clear that in order to progress through the various levels at the facility to gain additional privileges, our daughter would be required to participate in family sessions and to initiate contact on her call days. This was quite a switch. We had been calling her nearly every day, but now the responsibility would be hers. In addition, the other family members and friends on the contact list were restricted until she demonstrated some progress in therapy. Over the next couple months, the tone of the family counseling sessions transitioned from holding our daughter accountable for her actions and understanding the impact on the family unit to putting the family unit under a microscope.

"When did the family breakdown occur? She has a tremendous amount of hostility toward you as parents. There must be a root to all this hostility."

We don't know. We honestly don't know. Reflecting on 17 years of parenting this child, she has always been angry about something. The closest thing we can pin-point to an increase of anger was the incident at school when she threatened to kill another student, ultimately leading us to finding counseling services for her. The family sessions continued. During one session, our daughter admitted to inappropriate sexual contact with her sister; however, she claimed that she was asked to do those things and that it was consensual. Previously in acute care, she had confessed everything but the choking, but recanted. This wasn't the confession we had hoped for, but as the counselor said, it was an important step. It was something.

Within a couple weeks of the confession, which had provided a little hope that she might be making progress, the counselor canceled our family session, stating that she would rather confer with the grandparents that week to gain some perspective. We were caught off guard and agreed to her request. The outcome was a new focus on my pregnancy as the cause of the breakdown of the family unit. A grandparent reported that I had pre-eclampsia during my pregnancy and dealt with post-partum depression afterward. This was not new information, but for some reason became the focus in the weeks to come.

During another family session, our daughter read something from her journal. She told us again about the girl who touched her inappropriately on top of her clothes. This was not new information. We had heard this before during crisis counseling and it was dealt with appropriately. She claimed that this girl talked to her and our other daughter about kissing and make-out sessions with her boyfriend, and that she shouldn't have told them that. (The girls were ages 12, 14, and 16.) Don't most girls tell their friends about kissing boys? She then spoke of a boy who visited our neighbors. She snuck out on a walk with him, and he put his hand down her pants, but that it was consensual. Okay, so she had some activity we weren't aware of; however, he didn't penetrate her and it was consensual. While the disclosure of these events was a little concerning, we didn't hear anything about physical abuse or trauma. Nevertheless, the counselor indicated that because of the sexual behaviors that had transpired, treatment would precede from the standpoint of a victim. Many people who abuse are victims and she wanted to get to the root of the issue. Was there more the counselor knew and wasn't telling? Did she really feel that the events described above were abuse?

The counselor asked us to explain our feelings concerning what our daughter disclosed. My husband spoke first, reiterating what we have stated from the beginning. "We are truly sorry that this happened to you." What else is there to say? The story concerning the girl who was inappropriate has changed more frequently than a teenager changes clothes in a day. The allegations she has made about this individual have been all over the map, lack details, and she has no emotion when making the claims. Besides, the psychiatrist at the out-patient facility didn't believe her because of the lack of detail, changing story, inconsistent time frame, and total lack of emotion when discussing what she considered to be abuse. She also alleges that this girl abused our younger daughter and that they were forced to participate in sexual acts against their will for hours at a time. Our youngest daughter denies these claims and insists that the neighbor girl protected her from her sister. Furthermore, they were never alone with this individual for hours at a time for these events to have taken place. Again, we were pressed to give an authentic response and express our feelings about what she had disclosed. It was my turn. I didn't know what to say, other than to be truthful, so I explained that I was confused and didn't know how to express what I was feeling. I asked a few questions to clarify if the interaction with the boy was in fact consensual. We ended the session and both my husband and I felt as if our responses were deemed inappropriate by the counselor.

We were notified the following week that the case would be transferred back to the original counselor because of changes in staffing and reassignment of multiple cases. We expressed the need for a private conversation with the counselor to discuss diagnosis and the impending changes. She indicated that she really didn't have much time, but would try to call at a specific time the following day. She didn't call. I called and left a message, leaving specific times and numbers where I could be reached. Unfortunately, cell service is not available during my drive home. When I regained cell service 45 minutes later, she had called and left a message stating that she really only had a few minutes and could only speak with me if I could return her call in the next 15 minutes before she left for the day. That was after 4:00; our call was scheduled at 3:00. I called and left a message for her regarding call times and that we really wanted to speak with her as soon as possible. I called again the next morning. I also placed a call to the counselor who was to take over the case the next week and left a message. I called our insurance case manager to discuss the changes. I needed to talk to someone. The insurance case manager returned my call first. He was as perplexed as we were concerning the transition of treatment from having perpetrated against someone else to that of a victim. He assured me that his supervisor, a psychiatrist, would follow up with the psychiatrist at the facility and get back with me. Later that day, the counselor returned my call. Our conversation was lengthy and mostly unpleasant.

"I guess you have some questions?"

I expressed our concern that diagnosis hadn't been discussed in months and we hadn't heard anything further from either psychiatrist. I also explained that we were somewhat confused as to why treatment would shift to the standpoint of a victim. She explained that diagnosis was out of her hands, but that she didn't feel it should be necessary. We just need to focus on her behavior. She then brought up the responses my husband and I gave in the previous session. She claimed we did not give an appropriate response to the trauma our daughter disclosed. We were too clinical and "text book-y" in our replies. The feeling conveyed was that we were saying the right things, but we truly didn't believe trauma occurred. We were failing to "meet her half way." I explained that we had the other side of the story from our youngest. We could not overlook our personal experiences with our oldest daughter's history of lying. Nothing our oldest daughter had said, from the first allegation, through multiple changes of the story, to the present, made sense. It didn't add up. According to the counselor, that didn't matter. The victim's side of the story didn't matter, and we should focus only on what our oldest daughter was saying. We were not providing the proper emotional support. Why should our daughter want to speak with us if we don't believe her? Why should she ever confess to what happened, when the case had been dropped by the police and CPS? What benefit was there for her to tell the truth and admit to those behaviors? **If we really believed that she committed the acts against her sister, why didn't we press charges? It shouldn't matter that she is our daughter. We would have pressed charges if anyone else had committed those acts.**

Really? They are both our children. If someone else had committed these acts, yes, we would have pressed charges. However, we don't want to ruin her future. We didn't want her to go to juvenile detention or possibly worse, if the strangulation was taken into account. We wanted her to get help. We wanted her to go to a residential facility because sex offenders can be rehabilitated at a young age. Was this the right decision? I'm not certain. I see no evidence that this facility is willing or able to help. I fear that the "treatment" she is receiving here has no accountability for her actions and only looks for a way to justify what she has done, while collecting a hefty sum of insurance money.

According to the counselor, by law, our oldest is not a sex offender. We didn't have physical evidence or legal charges to indicate such. Regardless of definition, she committed an offense. Doesn't that matter? What about the statement of the victim and the fact that her story matches our memories of bruises and marks that didn't make sense at the time? The victim hid the truth with stories of hitting her arm on the fence to explain bruises and red marks, said she was sore from riding horses when I noticed a change in her gait and that she carried her body differently. My husband and I both saw an unexplainable red rash on her neck that corresponds with the time of the choking. All of these things line up with the time line of abuse presented in writing to authorities and her therapist. What about the lived experiences of the parents for 17 years and the history we can unfold? Doesn't any of that matter?

Apparently not. All that matters is self-proclaimed innocence of the perpetrator.

The conversation transitioned to point directly at me to explain the apparent breakdown of the family unit. My pregnancy was the topic. Yes, I had pre-eclampsia toward the end of my pregnancy. I'm not sure why this is relevant. I also experienced post-partum depression after giving birth. According to the counselor, this is where the problem began. I didn't bond with her properly, and she found other positive female role models in her grandmothers. (Isn't this insinuating that I am not only a bad mother for not bonding properly, but now I'm also not a positive female role model?) I bonded differently with my other child; therefore, the oldest had reason to be jealous. At the disclosure of abuse, I clearly chose one child over the other, as the youngest remained at home and we sought alternative living arrangements during outpatient treatment and then sent her to a residential facility. She hurled these statements for several minutes in an authoritative and patronizing tone, and then covered it all with a simple statement: "I'm not saying these things are true, but that is how your daughter must feel."

Even if she didn't mean those statements personally and is trying to justify my child's actions and emotions, it still doesn't make sense. Could the difference in infant-mother bonding be the root of jealously and resentment? I guess so. But what about the years of parenting, memory making, baking cookies, movies, shopping, talks, vacations and attending various award ceremonies, banquets, games, concerts, band competitions, etc.? It sounds as if we didn't provide equally for both children and purposely shunned the oldest while showering the youngest in some sort of glory. If the months of post-partum depression I experienced could cause my child to abuse another human being years later because she didn't bond properly as an infant, what about all those who are abandoned by their mother to live with their father, have parents who abuse drugs or alcohol leaving them unable to care for their children, are left in a garbage bin to be found by a stranger or those left in the hospital for adoption? Do all of those individuals grow to abuse others? If she had been successful in fatally choking her sister, would post-partum depression be to blame for murder? How dare you dismiss her actions by insinuating post-partum depression as the cause for all of her mental and emotional problems?

Apparently we had our hopes set too high in our attempt to get her the help she needed. It appeared as though we were reaching another dead end without answers. What do we do if they discharge her in three months and things are the same? She won't be able to live at home for the safety of our youngest. Is there no hope? Why is there no attempt at diagnosis? According to the new DSM, diagnosis could be given as young as 16. If their policy was to not diagnose any mental health issue prior to 18, why wasn't that disclosed prior to admission? What is to become of our family? How do we move forward?

Our experience with residential care ended after only four months of what should have been a six to nine month stay, with little notice that our daughter would be discharged so that we could make new living arrangements. According to the counselor, our daughter had met the requirements of the program by admitting to being present, participation in sexual acts, and acknowledging that she shouldn't have engaged in sexual behaviors with her sibling. That's it....no remorse, no admittance of coercion or abuse, no analysis into her behavior or attempt to diagnose the personality disorder believed to be present. She was present, she participated, and it shouldn't have happened. Once again, I felt as if the true victim was re-victimized and our family thrown under the bus. Our oldest was provided with nothing more than a pat on the back, discharge papers, a serious case of head lice that had been ongoing for nearly a month, and good luck. She didn't pose a problem in residential care or have violent behaviors toward the staff; therefore, she didn't fit the mold of the typical client in the facility. We inquired about having her moved to a different facility, but the counselor insisted that she didn't need further treatment. She met the requirements and there was nothing more to be done.

Now what?

Chapter 13: Redefining Family and Setting Boundaries

Nothing could have prepared us for the lack of treatment our oldest received in residential care or her sudden return. Once again, everything was turned upside down in an instant. Where would she live? What about school? (She had no real credits to transfer from residential care.) How do we protect our youngest? How will she feel and cope with all of the transition? It seemed life had more questions than answers. We examined all possibilities and determined that it would be in everyone's best interest if our oldest returned to her godfather's house until something else could be arranged. It had been a good short-term solution previously. We hoped to maintain our relationships with everyone involved and define a new normal during the few months that remained before she turned 18.

We had to quickly lay ground rules and set boundaries with our oldest and the surrounding family that lived across the road. The physical, mental, and emotional welfare of our youngest had to be the first priority. It seemed simple. Our oldest would not be permitted near the house without our prior approval. We would ensure that she was able to visit grandparents, extended family members, neighbors, and have time to ride her horse on a regular basis. No other family members were to schedule events on the premises without first discussing the proposed plans with us. In turn, we would assess each situation and make the decision that would be in the best interest of everyone involved. When it worked, it worked well. However, the best laid plans are often foiled by the interference of others. It didn't take long for family members to overstep the boundaries. Of course, they claimed forgetfulness. We reiterated the rules and boundaries, explained the reasoning behind our decision, smoothed out the wrinkles created by interference, and moved forward.

Moving forward frequently felt like walking through land mines in the dark. We never knew where the next explosion would occur. Every step had the possibility of being the wrong one that could bring further loss. Together, we could discuss and carefully plan our steps to avoid further destruction. However, when someone didn't respect the boundaries, chaos and turmoil ensued. These moments stressed our relationship as a couple, put undue stress on my husband, and continually upset all parties involved.

Tip: If you are a family member/friend close to the situation, respect the rules and boundaries. Your "forgetfulness" demonstrates total disregard for the victim and disrespect of our role as parents. You can't rush the healing process by forcing togetherness.

Our neighbors had always been friendly, but it didn't take long before their demeanor changed completely. Instead of the typical smile, wave, and conversation, their disposition was cold, hard, and included total avoidance of our youngest. My husband paid them a visit to see what was going on and to ensure they knew the ground rules for visitation at the present time. What should have been a casual conversation quickly turned into much more. They informed him that we had treated our oldest unfairly. Our oldest had told them part of what had happened. Knowing the extent our oldest child lies, he inquired about their "knowledge." Of course, she had spun another web of lies that placed her as the golden child, her sister as the enemy, and we were the devil incarnate. As carefully as he could, without divulging the details, my husband told them the truth of what happened. They sat in his face, denied that she would have done such things, made excuses for her behavior (if she in fact did wrong), and insinuated our youngest was lying. If anything had happened, someone else in the family must have been abusing our oldest to have caused this.

Once again, we were left dumbfounded that normal, intelligent, functioning adults were able to ignore the truth. Not only were they willing to overlook the truth, but they were overzealous to reject the truth and accept a lie. How in the world can anyone automatically assume the victim is completely lying, in spite of our lived experiences, therapy, psychological evaluations, and medical documentation? What friendship was once there quickly disappeared as they continually rejected us and our youngest while flaunting pictures of the oldest on social media about what a wonderful girl she was and how proud they were of her. Don't misunderstand, we are glad she has people in her life who are proud of her and are her friends. She needs that. But to knowingly side with a perpetual liar who raped and attempted to murder her sibling was more than we could handle. Those who are willing to blatantly ignore the truth in order to paint a rose colored image through the distorted lens provided by our oldest and not accept what happened, were never our friends to begin with.

My mother always said that opinions are like armpits; everyone has them, and all of them stink from time to time. The stinkin' thinking and opinions of others came from all directions once again. Extended family members from out of state began nosing around. Of course the rumor mill churned at warp speed and generated further problems. At first, we tried to ignore the comments from the peanut gallery. People will talk, regardless of what they know or think they know. However, those who continually pursued private information and bashed our decisions based on false information were corrected. These types of actions, along with the knowledge that our oldest resumed her normal activity of telling falsehoods about us to people far and wide continued to erode relationships.

The most difficult was the loss of "Uncle Matt." After a few months of her being in his home, he believed that she was doing tremendously better because he provided daily devotions and spiritual accountability. Because we cautioned him that we had seen the spiritual transformation before, he began to distance himself. Not too long after, we learned that our oldest had been sneaking around, booked, and checked into a local hotel, although she was not of age and while living in his home. When questioned about the charges on her bank account, she told elaborate lies of how she had lost her debit card, ordered a new one, and had no idea how the charges were made for 20-30 minutes. I finally confronted her with the evidence we had from surveillance footage. She showed no remorse for her actions and excused the incident as a desire for more privacy to video chat with someone. I can't imagine that an individual with a part-time, minimum wage job spends over $100 to video chat. Needless to say, I found this all very concerning. What was she getting herself into? Was she meeting with strangers? Was she involved in prostitution? Would her behavior lead her into abusive situations or worse, sex slavery? So I took her phone for the day to look for leads. As she handed it across the table, she informed me that I wouldn't find anything. She conducted all of her online happenings in secret mode. (Why use secret mode unless you have something to hide?)

I spoke with "Matt" about the issue. He assured me he would speak with her about it and get back with me. After a week, I contacted him to find out how their talk had gone. He stated that she had told him a similar story of going to the hotel to video chat. When I asked if he believed her, his response let me know that our relationship with him was probably forever severed. "What choice do I have but to believe her?" He had no issue with her willingness to blatantly lie about the situation and lack of remorse for lying or concern for her actions. I was shocked at his gullibility. He chose to believe her new found spiritual charade, rather than deal with reality. It was more comfortable for him to believe a falsehood than to realize that her spirituality was superficial and that daily devotions weren't enough to stop the lies. He needed to believe that his efforts were heroic and effective, but a zebra doesn't change its stripes. Because of his willingness to believe lies, cold nature toward our youngest, and the ever growing distance between us, we watched him walk out of our lives completely. The grief was an incredibly heavy burden, especially for our youngest. After all, he was the person she had trusted enough to tell, and he had been the one to sit with her while we attended family counseling sessions with our oldest. She had officially lost one of the most important people in her life because her sister managed to pull the wool over his eyes.

The fact is, people will believe what they want to believe. If information is presented as an emotional appeal by a convincing manipulator, most will defend the lie in spite of the revealed truth. I can't change this. I can't run ahead and provide a warning. Before she turned 18, I felt obligated to do so in order to protect others. When I learned that our oldest was becoming active in children's ministry at her new church and was even babysitting, I contacted the pastor to ensure he was aware of the potential danger. His responded by stating that they had safeguards in place at the church. As much as I want to warn others so that no harm may come to their children, I cannot. As much as I want to defend myself, my husband, and our youngest, it is impossible. Instead, I daily choose to hold my head high, fully accepting the reality of what our oldest has done to our youngest, and face the stares, whispers, avoidance, awkward silence, and unsolicited opinions of others with boldness. Although we cannot defend ourselves from defamation of character, I refuse to sink into the shadows of shame cast by another. I will not hide for fear of judgement from those who do not know the truth or reject the truth to embrace a lie. I will never stop protecting with every fiber of my being. I will never stop caring for our children. The decisions, actions, and opinions of others do not define who I am as a wife, mother, daughter, teacher, or woman. We have and will continue to establish boundaries with family, friends, and outsiders as the need arises. We will protect our own and move forward, with our without the approval of others. At the end of the day, all that matters is that we know we have done our best with the resources we have to protect, guide, nurture, and bring wholeness.

Chapter 14: How to Friend 101

Our journey has been filled with an astounding amount of "dumb shit." However, there were also helpful and validating statements made by friends, family members, co-workers, and strangers who became our heroes. My husband and I walked this journey together, yet our experiences are unique. While he had support from friends and family at times, I felt very isolated and lonely. At one point, a mutual friend approached my husband and said that she was praying for us, but that it wasn't enough. She wanted to be a friend to me, but she didn't know how. She asked him what she could do, but he was caught off guard and wasn't sure what to say. I had stayed home from church that day with our youngest who was severely struggling and couldn't go out. Although I knew she was a good friend, I was a little surprised to find out that I wasn't as invisible as I felt and that someone cared enough to ask.

At one point, a Facebook friend asked, "Where is your support system? When we went through a crisis with one of our children, a few friends really stepped up to the plate and provided a respite once a week or once a month to provide some normalcy to our lives." Apparently, I don't know people like that. She tried to assure me that I did, and that I only needed to let a few people know of our situation and help would surely be on the way. Sadly, I was right; I don't know people like that. Friends, even those who knew some of the details, became distant. I guess this type of tragedy is too much for others to face. It must be like driving past a gruesome accident on the interstate. You can see it's horrible, carnage is visible, and you are thankful that you get to keep driving and let the murky details of what little you saw in passing fade into the distance of the rear view mirror as you continue toward your destination. While you feel bad for those who were affected, you are grateful it wasn't you or yours.

Along the way, many people said, "Let me know if there is anything I can do." But I didn't know what to tell them. I didn't know how to ask for help. I felt like if someone wanted to do something, they would just do it. I've done things for people during difficult times without being asked. Wouldn't others do the same? When things were first revealed, I wanted to tell them the truth. I'm lonely, embarrassed, confused, and angry. Do I really need to say I could use a friend? But I was uncertain and wary to trust others. I was exhausted by my own emotions and didn't have the stamina to risk judgement or rejection. Eventually, I found strength to send a text or make a call asking for relief, but most of the time, I sat in silence and wondered if anyone would be there if I called for help. I understand that a crisis makes most people uncomfortable, but please don't allow feeling awkward to keep you from showing your concern. There are many ways to show you care, most are simple, and many don't require financial resources or much time.

1. Listen to understand, not to reply. There is no quick fix to our situation. Things won't simply return to "normal." Understand that this is a long journey that we must walk. We need to be heard, not talked at or treated like a puzzle that must be solved.

2. Send a text or private message. This only takes a few seconds of your time, but it means the world. It doesn't have to be much. A simple, "Thinking of you today." is better than not reaching out. If you are a person of faith, text a quick, "Praying for you." Better yet, text what you are praying that day. A few people did this, and I read and re-read those prayers over and over. They offered hope during some of the darkest moments when I felt totally alone.

3. Ask how I am and want a real answer, not the generic "okay" I give to the masses.

4. Ask about our youngest. Many people only focused on the well-being of our oldest child that I became angry and resentful when the first question was about her. The life of our youngest child has been forever changed, she suffers with PTSD and is the victim in this situation, yet she is often invisible to others and rarely asked about.

5. Set a time for us to meet. "Can I take you out for coffee/ice cream? Would you like to go for a walk or just sit at the lake?" Insist. I feel guilty to take time aside for self-care, but I really need it.

6. Movie night in. We don't have to talk about the crisis. Popcorn, cheap pizza, or just the movie, I would love anything that breaks the routine. It's the fact that you are taking time to provide comfort with your presence that means the most.

7. Tell me about your life. Be real. If you are struggling with something, talk to me like you normally would. Although you might feel that it is "adding a burden" to me while we are going

through enough already, it helps bring balance and takes my mind off of our situation. It's not a burden. It's good to be needed.

8. Provide a meal. Frozen lasagna is good! You don't have to be a great cook. During the immediate crisis, we were constantly on the road and cooking was a chore. While we were redefining life, emotions ran high and we were all frequently too exhausted to care about preparing food.

9. Don't forget we are married. Offer a date night. Help us protect our marriage. Believe me, our relationship is stressed to the max. We need time to be adults, look into each other's eyes, and remember that we are truly in this together every step of the way.

10. Gift cards. It doesn't have to be much or anything fancy. This is helpful for many reasons. Much time is spent on the road all the time with doctor appointments, counseling appointments, and trips to a residential facility out of state. Even with good insurance, the out of pocket expense is staggering. Gift cards are an excellent way to help. Even a $10.00 gift card to McDonalds is helpful.

11. If our relationship is close enough that you visit my home, I'm thankful for your willingness to overlook the clutter. My youngest needs a lot of extra time right now. Sometimes I spend hours sitting with her on the couch or holding her during times when she wants to stop living. My house doesn't matter during those times. Donating 10 minutes to help run the vacuum, unload the dishwasher, or wipe down the bathroom sink is practical and helps lighten the load.

12. If you are a significant person in my youngest child's life, young or old, please don't forget her. She really needs you right now. I know it's awkward and you don't know what to say, but treat her normally. No one expects you to try to fix this. When you help her by displaying kindness, you help me.

Even when tragedy strikes, life goes on for everyone. I understand that. No one can be there as a support all the time; that's not expected. But if you consider yourself a friend, be there. Take time. Make time. It only takes a few seconds to show that you care with a text message, and those little messages mean the world. You won't regret doing the right thing.

Chapter 15: Encouragement, Validation, and Practicality

Some of the most validating statements we received came from those who were originally strangers, but became our life line. At the original disclosure, a crisis counselor provided much needed validation.

"I'm so sorry this has happened, but you are doing the right thing. It would be wrong to look the other way and pretend this didn't happen. This is the lancing. It's ugly and very painful, but this is the first step to healing. It's a slow process. Remember that your oldest child has done this to herself. You didn't cause this. Don't blame yourself. Your youngest child didn't do anything to cause the abuse or to deserve it, and she needs your love and support more than anything. The safety of your youngest child must be your number one priority. You are doing what's best for both of your children."

Thank you. Thank you for knowing the horrible details of our family and not passing judgement. Thank you for not assuming that we are bad parents. Thank you for acknowledging that our oldest child is the one who committed unspeakable acts and our youngest is the victim. Thank you for telling me that we are doing the right thing by facing this brutal reality and taking action. Thank you. This stranger lightened the load during our conversation and continually reminded me that we made the right decision by not sweeping this under the rug, as many do. We needed to seek help and protect our youngest child at all costs. I cried tears of frustration, anger, agony, regret, and shame with a total stranger. She carried our burden with us. She provided contact information for resources that would prove invaluable. Most importantly, she was truly compassionate. For this dear lady, her job was not just her job. She truly cared about people and about us. She followed up via phone and text message long after the general course of action and ensured that we were getting the support services needed. Although I didn't ever get to meet her and only know her first name, I will forever be grateful for her kindness.

When she said it was a slow process, like the healing of a wound, I thought I understood the analogy at the time. With a physical wound, if infection sets in and an area must be lanced, the healing process can be lengthy. There isn't a quick fix. This injury doesn't need a Band-Aid or even some gauze, tape, and antibiotic ointment. If not treated properly, the infection will recur and potentially spread, causing further damage, and potentially, death. Proper treatment requires removal of the infection, complete cleansing, and sterile packing so that the wound can heal from the inside out. Regular care must be provided and the packing removed a little at a time to ensure proper healing. Such is the case when this type of devastation is discovered in a family. The victim is the most severely wounded; however, each member of the family is affected and requires careful care to heal the mind, heart, and emotions. Just as a physical wound requires care and attention to heal properly, we must heal from the inside out.

As we sat in the emergency room hallway, waiting for oldest to be admitted, our pastor acknowledged the truth.

"Today is the worst day of your life, but you'll look back and it will be the best. When truth is revealed, the healing can begin."

And a few days later...

"I know you're numb. You can't even pray right now. It's our time to carry you through this. There is no wrong way for you to feel at the moment."

Wow. We weren't expected to be "Super Christians" or to pull ourselves up by the bootstraps. We were allowed to be broken. There was no other way we could be, and that was acceptable. We didn't have to be strong, brave, or even hopeful. We were allowed to just be. He understood that just getting up every day and putting one foot in front of the other was all we could do, and that was enough. He provided wisdom, a listening ear, and much prayer over the months ahead. We're still waiting to look back and see that as the best day of our lives, but we know that the days would have been much darker had the truth not been revealed at that time. We were broken, but we were alive. Somehow, we would heal.

I called a dear friend.

"I won't say I know how you feel because I don't. I can't imagine the heartbreak. I'm so sorry. I just don't know what to say. I'm speechless."

She was speechless, and that was okay. She was in shock, much as we were. How could this have happened to our family? Even though she is a mother and understands heartbreak over children, she was wise enough to not attempt to compare hardships. There is no comparison, even if events had been similar. Heartbreak is a unique experience, especially when the heart has been shattered. Thank you dear friend. You didn't have much to say that night, but it was enough. You felt my pain. You didn't pass judgement on me or my children. You prayed for me. You cared.

I received incredible support from my doctor, her nurses, and the support system found at HOPE for months to come. The messages were similar, heartfelt, and wise.

"You've done everything you can do as a parent. Every system designed to help has failed you."

"Are you protecting your marriage? Personal or even couples counseling would be helpful, but right now you need to get your bearings. I understand that right now it would just be extra stress, but promise you will take care of yourself and find time for your marriage through all this."

"You guys are doing such an incredibly hard, but also such an incredibly important thing by getting your oldest daughter help. If you don't try to change her mind set about her behaviors so she sees how wrong her actions are, it's hard to tell what she would do later in life."

One nurse even shared her personal experience with PTSD and that of her son. She gave practical insight for daily survival and reminded me to always celebrate the small achievements. Two counselors shared their stories of abuse and panic attacks. I was awe struck at the humanity of these professionals to tell of their own struggles and offer encouragement. They didn't have to do that, but each felt if her experience would help me or my family, it was worth sharing.

At work, a few of our closest co-workers/friends knew the truth and provided support and encouragement to each of us along the way. They didn't ask probing questions, but expressed concern for each of us and the girls on a regular basis. I missed a teacher training and a couple meetings, but a fellow teacher kept me up to date on the necessary information and would send reminders of important dates, knowing that I had more important things on my mind.

When it came to practical assistance, family came through.

Although time is precious, those who found time for text messages, calls, lunch, and were willing to sit and have normal conversation, no conversation, or allow venting without judgement or suggestions provided much needed relief.

At first, we were on the road every day to the hospital for one child and multiple appointments for the other. Some family offered financial support and we declined. We didn't want to need help or feel indebted. Others were adamant. "Here. You need this, now and later. You don't need financial stress on top of everything else. You have extra travel expenses, bills, meals, etc. It's a gift, not a loan." They were right. We did need the financial help, both at that moment, and later when large co-pays and extensive travel were required. I'm not sure what we would have done without their generosity. We will be paying for expenses incurred for quite some time.

When there is a crisis, those who are going to respond generally do so when the tragedy occurs. This is critical. However, a select few understood that the depth of our crisis would take time to heal. These individuals remained resolute in providing validation, friendship, and an occasional respite during the many months ahead. For those who were willing to weather the storm and walk alongside of us for miles, thank you. Your compassion and consideration are priceless.

Chapter 16: A Mother's Emotions and Flailing Faith

The emotional rollercoaster that I was involuntarily strapped onto, while the tracks were burning, was inescapable. Shock quickly gave way to anger. Most view anger as a negative emotion; however, in this case, anger enabled me to complete the difficult tasks that had to be done right away. My anger quickly spread from total outrage that my oldest could have done this, to being angry at myself for not noticing the warning signs sooner. Of course, hind sight is 20/20 and I could now see the writing on the wall that I hadn't noticed before. Shame, blame, and guilt joined the party, fueling anger, and were assisted by the insensitivity of several in the mental health profession, friends, and family members. While these emotions plagued my heart and mind for months, none were as difficult to process as grief. Unbelievable grief for all that had been lost for our family unit would erupt spontaneously. Taking our youngest through the forensic interview process, to counseling appointments, watching as she lost all of her friends and even her relationship with the single adult she trusted enough to tell first, watching the self-doubt grow as she questioned if she would ever be good enough for anyone to fall in love with, guiding her through academic struggles, witnessing her own anger and grief at the toll the abuse had taken on her body, and the times she battled depression to stay alive just one more day were constant reminders that we could be grieving the physical loss of our baby. This realization of what could have been brought deep gratefulness that she broke the silence, giving herself the opportunity to live. Thankfully, I did not have to grieve the death of my child. Instead, I grieved for the living.

Most of the time, grief is associated with death; however, in a metaphorical sense, our family died that dreaded day in September. Grieving for the living is unconventional, but very real. When someone you love suddenly becomes something you didn't expect or chooses unacceptable patterns of behavior, it is a tremendous loss. Grief is a natural response.

I grieved for our oldest. She transformed from a challenging child into someone we feared had serious mental health issues. Her personal struggles transformed her into someone who committed unspeakable acts against her sister that could have warranted a juvenile detention and/or a criminal record, if the law had taken things seriously. Her future changed quickly. She would no longer graduate high school with honors, attend her senior prom, or attend ministerial school as she had planned. These were no longer options. Instead, she completed the GED and found minimum wage employment.

I grieved for your youngest. Once a seemingly confident, fun-loving child had transformed into a withdrawn, depressed, and anxiety ridden teenager before our eyes. It was a slow process at first, but after disclosure of the abuse the depression and anxiety magnified as the symptoms of PTSD came into view. So much was lost for our youngest. The damage to her body, emotions, and mind were beyond comprehension. I grieved for what had been lost during the two years of abuse. I grieved for what was lost in the present as she walked each step unsteadily, while I prayed for answers and wholeness. I grieved for the struggles that could yet come in the future. I grieved for the loss of concentration and confidence as she worked hard to complete assignments in 9th grade, knowing that she still had three more years of high school, and hopefully would be ready to attend college afterwards. I grieved alongside of her as she lost every friend she ever had and attempted to forge new friendships. I grieved as her godparent became distant and even more when she stated that she felt as if she no longer had an uncle. I grieved with her and her doctor as the report was read to us concerning the damage to her body, knowing that this was only the tip of the iceberg relating to the mental and emotional scars that were hidden, and again when it was discovered that the trauma triggered other physical issues in the midst of what was already hell. I grieved, as most parents do, as their child experiences their first break-up; however, it put the spotlight on all of her insecurities that no one would ever want her because she wasn't good enough. I grieved as her anxiety and depression kept her socially behind bars. She no longer wanted to go shopping, eat out, or see the movie she had waited months to be released in theaters. Would she recover? Would she regain confidence and not live the life of a victim? Would she overcome her personal insecurities and fears to discover the wonderful, amazing, and strong woman she is?

At times, I grieved for myself. These short lived moments were full of hot, angry tears that seemed to spring forth unannounced and came from a never ending source. I had to navigate the stages of grief, denial, anger, bargaining, depression and acceptance. Each person processes loss differently. Some go through all of the stages of grief, while others do not.

The stages are not linear; they are recursive and complicated, especially when experiencing unconventional grief. I bypassed denial and didn't do much bargaining, but anger and depression were my constant companions.

I also grieved for what I saw as a lack of faith. In the Christian community, we are continually reminded to trust God, have faith, and just believe. We are encouraged to "dig deep" into the wells of our faith and salvation. We are told that in times of despair we only need to "run to the mountain," stay in the Word, pray, worship, and continue to fight the good fight. But I couldn't. I withdrew out of anger. Not only was I angry at our circumstances, but I was angry with God. On some level, I felt that I shouldn't have a right to be angry with God, but I couldn't shake it. Our life, as we knew it, had imploded. We had raised our kids according to the principles of the Bible, prayed over them from before conception, and yet here we were. What had we done wrong? I felt as though God had betrayed me. I did all I knew to do to guide, direct, and protect my children. We kept a careful balance between family and ministry life; our kids always came first, not church activities. We trusted that God would keep what we had committed to Him. I felt that God let down on His end of the bargain. I felt betrayed. In addition to feeling betrayed, I felt guilty for experiencing that emotion. After all, God never leaves us or forsakes us, right? How could I feel this way and be a Christian? Had I inadvertently turned my back on God during tragedy? Had I lost my faith? Why couldn't I find any resolution or peace? Where was God in any of this?

Although I had been taught that Jesus experienced every emotion that we could experience, I experienced guilt of feeling spiritually abandoned and betrayed. I finally realized that I wasn't alone in this emotion either. Even Jesus felt this way concerning his heavenly father. Jesus had lived a sinless life, understanding his purpose and destiny for the salvation of mankind, yet while enduring the agony of the cross questioned why God had forsaken him. It was a liberating moment. If Jesus could give up his life feeling abandoned and betrayed by God, I could experience these emotions without guilt or shame. Even during all of the questioning and feelings of spiritual abandonment, I knew that although I didn't understand my own thoughts and emotions, God knew exactly where I was. Grappling with faith was difficult. I finally came to the conclusion that I need not experience guilt or shame about my emotions, even the way I felt about my faith. God was big enough to handle my anger, and it was okay to be honest about how I felt. (After all, He knew anyway.)

Little by little, I made peace with my spiritual distress, found acceptance in the fact that our family was forever changed, and understood that I need not look for what I believed was "normal" ever again. We would redefine the definition of boundaries within the family and forge a new "normal" that would have to be unconventional. The solutions to these issues would not be a sitcom or Hallmark movie. I didn't know how things would turn out in the end; all I knew is that I must not give up every effort to protect and care for my children. I would help the oldest as much as she would allow to find independence, and I would give my life to protect and help the youngest regain a sense of self, confidence, hope, and wholeness.

Negative emotions were never hard to find and it was easy to feel overwhelmed by circumstances at home, but I was determined to celebrate the little things. We celebrated with our oldest as she completed the GED requirements and got her first job. We celebrated when our youngest was able to walk in the school building. We celebrated when she was able to attend class for longer than 15 minutes. We celebrated when she was able to go shopping or out to dinner. We celebrated discovering and experiencing emotions, even the painful ones. On really bad days, we celebrated getting out of bed and facing another day. We celebrated the will to live, love, and laugh again by getting matching semicolon tattoos. We celebrated small milestones along my dissertation journey that were only significant because of the circumstances in which they were completed. We celebrated things that others take for granted...safety, learning to live at home without fear, completing a school year, and the journey to personal acceptance.

One of the greatest game changers and sources of happiness came with four paws, fur, beautiful brown eyes, and a smile that is contagious. Because of the severity of her symptoms, the recommendation of her doctor and therapist, wisdom of the judge, and the generosity of the Crime Victims Compensation Fund, our youngest was provided with a service dog trained for PTSD. After several months of paper work and waiting, the request was approved and financial provision made for a service dog to become part of our family. I traveled with my youngest from east to west to meet her companion and train. I knew in my heart that a service dog would help her regain her life, but nothing could have prepared me for the transformation I witnessed once "Mini" took her left side. It was meant to be. From the time they met, they quickly bonded. I watched in amazement as my withdrawn and shy child talked to Elizabeth, the trainer, a complete stranger, and willingly went on a walk around the grounds without me.

The next day, we met in a public area to continue training. Within less than an hour, my daughter who had become fearful, plagued with panic attacks, and would not leave my side in public was walking through a store without me. As they continued to bond during the training, she started to regain her life. Her outlook became more positive, body language shifted from uncertain to gaining confidence, and she was ready to take on the outside world with her companion. During the few days we stayed in Tucson, we participated in more "normal" activities than she had been able to attempt in months. We went shopping, visited family, dined at several restaurants, and saw two movies at a local cinema. The emotions experienced when a mother sees her child begin to regain the life that had been stolen are beyond comprehension. Thankfully, Elizabeth understood. We smiled, laughed, and even cried happy tears together as we watched the dynamic duo form an inseparable bond that would transform our lives forever. I am eternally grateful for the investment made in my daughter's life.

The emotional roller coaster is never ending. We have highs, lows, twists, and many unexpected turns. I have experienced all of the emotions described and will continue to experience them as I move forward. It is a process. I have learned that I am allowed to experience each and every emotion as it comes. Not only is experiencing these emotions normal, but it is a healthy part of the healing process. Although I like to feel as though I am strong, I have learned that no person can handle everything in stride and that it is healthy to experience emotions, the good and the bad, and move forward. It is part of the human experience. Because I feel anger does not mean that I harbor un-forgiveness, or that I am a bad mother, Christian, or human being. When I celebrate the small things with one child, it does not mean I am rejecting or being neglectful to the other. When I take time for myself to grieve loss or to simply just be, I am not being selfish or self-centered. There are times that I am every emotion and others that I am devoid of emotion. Although emotions are powerful and impact my life, I am not controlled by my feelings. I am a good wife, mother, daughter, teacher, student, friend, and person. I am capable. I am intelligent. I am loving. I am reserved. I am confident. I am a warrior who will not run from the battle. I am. I am enough.

Chapter 17: For Better or Worse

It seems that in our culture, marriage is something that is easily cast aside when times get tough. But for us, divorce because of difficulty is not an option. Remaining happily married requires a conscious effort to put the needs of your spouse ahead of your own, regardless of life's circumstances. It requires compassion, empathy, and dedication to putting your relationship first when times in the midst of hardship and when people become intrusive. We knew that manipulation, unsolicited opinions, and the "helpful advice" from others could drive a wedge between us. In order to survive as a couple, we had to maintain open communication and weather the storm together.

Thoughts of my child being sexually assaulted haunted me in nightmares. Sex had always been an intimate and pleasurable experience with my husband, and suddenly my thoughts of intimacy were negative. I couldn't imagine the fear and pain my daughter had endured at the hands of someone else. The most intimate part of her body and life as a woman had been completely violated. The thought of sex became marred by what had happened. It was now distasteful, dirty, and disgusting. Because my husband and I are committed to open communication, I was completely honest. I was a little surprised when he said that he had been feeling the same way. We discussed the need to protect our marriage in all aspects. Face it, sex is an important part of marriage for most people. We gave it some time. But how do you move past images in your mind of your child being abused at the thought of a kiss or intimate caress? Slowly, with understanding, and open communication.

Differing work schedules impeded our efforts to even communicate at times, but we strategically made time to talk about what had happened, process where we were individually and as a family unit, assess the mental emotional state of our youngest, make decisions concerning upcoming events, speculate the mental status of our oldest and what we could do to assist her in finding independence and success, and determine how to handle the stress created by family members. Sometimes it seemed as if there was only one topic: damage control. However, a healthy relationship can't focus on the negative. In spite of it all, we made time to reconnect as a couple. We went out to dinner. Sometimes we just sat on the couch and watched movies. We made time for romance. We dared to dream again. Of course, our ultimate dream is that of wholeness for the family, but sometimes we needed to dream of other things...things for us. Whether it was in hopes of having a brief getaway to our favorite resort for our anniversary, one day owning a houseboat, or relocating to a new area with better jobs, a little privacy, and a fresh start, we dreamed together for our future as a family and as a couple.

Chapter 18: Continuing Care and the Future

I wish I could provide a conclusion to this story. However, this isn't a sitcom that can be neatly packaged in 30 minutes or even a movie that can have closure in a few hours. It's a journey. Our journey started in September 2016 and will continue for the rest of our lives. Each member of our household is on a personal journey, and we will move forward as a family on our corporate journey. We aren't sure what that will look like or what the future holds.

At the present, our oldest is out of residential care, living with her godparent, working, and taking a few classes at a career center. Yes, we help her. We incurred additional debt to provide her reliable transportation. We bought her a cell phone and pay for her plan. We helped her complete the task for the GED and take the ACT, if she decides to attend college. We have provided financial assistance, bought groceries, work clothes, and repair, maintenance, and new tires for her car. We take care of her entry fees to horse shows and include her in activities as much as we can. We go out for breakfast/lunch and go shopping, when she is willing to go. She is still our daughter, even when she is disrespectful and purposely hurtful, and even if we must have distance at times for the sake of peace, healing, and wholeness.

Our youngest is reclaiming her life and forming an identity separate from the abuse, one day at a time. Her service dog continues to be a tremendous asset and has enabled her to rejoin public activities and build confidence. She is becoming more successful at school and was recently inducted into the National Honor Society. She may struggle, but she will overcome in time with continued support and understanding.

As a couple, we're weathering the storm and are determined to come through stronger than ever. We dream of a better tomorrow. My husband maintains the most communication with our oldest, as she continues to blame me for everything and hates her sister. He also keeps a careful balance between our little family and those who continually pry and create drama. He protects the family unit and carefully weighs the pros and cons of every decision we make on our quest for healing.

Personally, I have resolved to try to do something so that another mother doesn't have to walk this journey feeling alone, afraid, and ashamed. I want more than anything to be the voice that brings about change. Can I change the system? Doubtful. Can I bring awareness on a larger scale? Probably not. But I can help alleviate the feelings of isolation to a mother's heart that has been shattered into a million pieces. I can be honest. We are the broken, but we will gather the shards and carefully place them together to create something beautiful.

What happened in our family is horrible. I wish I could turn back time and still have my current knowledge to prevent tragedy; however, that is impossible. I can't change the past. I can only impact the present and hope to shape the future. I will continue to make the best decisions I can to help my children in every way possible. I will pray for healing for our family unit, but I know this will take time, honesty, and faith. If sharing my story can help only one person, it is worth it.

Who decides which horrors are hidden and which are exposed? Who decides if I, other parents in a similar situation, or the abused must hide under the burden of guilt and shame? Some say society. I say no one will silence my voice. It is only through silence that the abuse continues and the victims remain vulnerable. Silence only increases suffering and generates unbearable isolation and despair. Will I be judged by what has happened? Will you decree that you would have done things better and that it could never happen in your home? Will you have a million suggestions as to what we could have/should have done or what we should do now? Probably. In fact, many will sit in judgement. Some will side with the perpetrator, regardless of the brutality that occurred or the honesty displayed through the sharing of truth. Some will say that if we would have just _____, things would be better. Fill in the blank with whatever you choose: been more strict/lenient, had more faith, been more/less protective, taken specific vitamins or health supplements, pressed the mental health/legal system more, or swept it all aside and pretend it didn't happen. I hope that mental health issues and abuse never knock at your door, but to say that it would never happen is presumptuous at best. To suggest that following any specific advice would have stopped the abuse from happening is only possible with hind sight, which is not possible, and removes the responsibility from the one individual who chose to exert her will to overpower another.

But to the dear parent who is suffering a similar fate, know that you are not alone. Take action. Protect the victim at all costs. Be the advocate for each child, the victim and the perpetrator. They need you. To those who walk this journey, I respectfully place a stone alongside yours in memory of all you have lost. Indeed, there is much to grieve, and we will not walk this journey alone or our struggle be forgotten.

Chapter 19: The Heart of a Husband and Father

As a Christian, I believe it is important to keep my priorities straight. After God, the person of most importance is my wife, followed closely by my children. I believe it is important to be a good husband and father. Over the years, I have done many things in service of the Lord, but my greatest calling is to be an example of a Godly man to my family. Much of my identity is as a husband and father, and the events of September 2016 shook everything I ever believed or thought myself to be.

It is difficult to describe the range of emotions experienced that terrible week that plunged my family into darkness. To suddenly find out the family I thought I had was a lie was a devastating blow. From the inception of our family, I prayed that sexual assault would not touch my wife or daughters. God created sex to be a beautiful thing between a husband and wife, and to be violated in such a personal and intimate way is something I had always hoped no one in my family would ever experience.

To find out that one of my children had been assaulted repeatedly, over the course of two years was devastating. It's bad enough to find out that one of your children has been harmed, but it is made worse by the knowledge that the harm and loss was perpetuated by your other child. I was instantly torn in two by conflicting emotions. All parents can probably understand the desire to protect and defend a hurting child. My youngest daughter had just revealed that she had been harmed in our home. Our efforts to protect our children had failed. We did not allow our children to run the roads or bounce from house to house with friends. In fact, they did not stay in homes of individuals unless we knew a great deal about the dynamics of the home. We knew where our children were and who they were with. We thought we were being careful. We thought we were keeping them safe. But we were wrong.

In any business organization the hardest threat to defend against is the one from the inside. The same can be said for the family. You can defend from the neighbor down the street much easier than from the person in the next room. We believed our oldest daughter had some psychological and emotional problems, we made many efforts to get her help, but all of our efforts were in vain. Professionals did not provide insight. In spite of my wife's best efforts to explain that something was amiss with our child, her concerns were dismissed time and time again. We were told that her behavior and emotional outbursts were normal for the age. That could have been true, but what we didn't know was the depth and darkness of her issues.

My faith was shaken. I was angry at God. Through years of ministry, I had told countless people that while people will let you down, God will never let you down. I felt like God had let me down. How could He allow this to happen? Not only do I have a daughter who is a victim of violent abuse, but I also have a daughter who is the abuser. How can I want justice for one, when that means hurting the other? I want a whole family, but I don't know if that can ever be restored. Where was God in any of this?

During the week after disclosure, I knelt down in front of our couch and told God that I didn't want to be angry at Him anymore. I cried and I prayed. I prayed and I cried. After some time, I felt the peace that only comes from above and knew in my heart that God was in control of the situation and that I would have my family back one day. I knew we had a long road to walk, but God had us in His hand. The months that followed were very dark, but I continued to experience peace. Every time it seemed we could not go on, I was reminded that God was not surprised or caught off guard by anything that had happened. In spite of tragedy, He is still God.

Jeremiah 29:11 says, "For I know the plans I have for you," declares the Lord, "plans to prosper you and not to harm you, plans to give you hope and a future." I want God's plans for my daughters. I have no trouble believing our youngest will walk in those plans. Although she has suffered terrible violence, she has been and will continue to be a survivor. I believe she will recover and become stronger than she ever believed possible. I want God's plans for our oldest daughter too. She has messed up her life. She has messed up her sister's life. She has messed up our family. Because of my love for her, I do not want true justice for what she has done. I want her to become a successful, productive, and upstanding citizen. I want her to find happiness. I hope that with God's help, she will eventually acknowledge what she has done, be remorseful, and be willing to get professional help for the mental health issues I believe are present.

Through this experience, I have learned a lot about myself and each member of our family. We have all learned a lot about ourselves as we walked each step of the journey. My wife and I dealt with things differently. We have different personalities and coping methods. Of course, we process things differently as men and women. She has struggled more, in some ways, than I have. She tends to be critical of herself and struggled to see that we couldn't have done things differently or better, unless we had prior knowledge of what was going to happen. Although we processed our grief and emotions differently, one way is no better than the other.

I would be lost without her strength. She is a woman of decisive action. While I might know what needs to be done, I tend to delay uncomfortable decisions and actions. She, however, is quick to take action, once we determine what needs to be done. I could not have navigated this situation and provided the emotional support our youngest child needed without her by my side. Outsiders have been mistaken in thinking she is cold or unfeeling, but they don't get to see what I see. She keeps her composure in public and only falls apart behind closed doors, within the safety of our home. They mistake her resolve and ability to make incredibly difficult decisions as uncaring. But she is anything but uncaring. She cares deeply and her love for both children is boundless and profound. She does not, however, allow love to cloud her vision and enter into denial. She will not sweep the actions of our oldest aside and neglect the needs of our youngest, the victim, for the sake of appearances. She will do anything that is necessary to protect our youngest and make her feel safe. She also loves our oldest and is willing to be hated by her for trying to get her the help she needs. Although she doesn't see it within herself, she is one of the strongest people I know and I applaud her efforts in trying to increase awareness to this dark issue. No one should judge the heart of a mother; you don't know the depths of love and anguish that come from the same heart. Few could walk her path.

If you are a parent walking this road through hell with your children, I encourage you to hold fast to your faith. It is the only thing that can calm your heart and mind, even though sometimes you just have to trust blindly and keep walking step by step. I also encourage you to invest time into your marriage. Don't allow stress, grief, manipulation, and the overwhelming needs that are present to create distance between you and your spouse. Your children will grow up and move on; you pledged your heart to your spouse for your lifetime. Go out to dinner. Hug often. Make time for romance. Plan for the future and don't be afraid to dream. Be intentional in expressing your love to each other.

If you are a friend or family member watching your loved ones walk the long road, be supportive, listen, and offer practical help. My wife has clearly outlined the common pit falls and insensitive statements made by others. Avoid these mistakes, and if you make one, be quick to apologize. Don't sit on the sidelines and wish you could do something to help. You can do something. Your support means a lot.

I would love to be able to write that we are better and my family is whole. Unfortunately, that is still not the case. The road to wholeness is an individual and family journey that will take time. I can say that we are better today than we were in September 2016, and with God's help, will continue to improve. The road to wellness is often difficult, and I fear that some relationships may deteriorate further before they improve. We are still waiting for God's complete work in our lives, but have peace in the knowledge that He is still God and He knows exactly where we are individually and as a family. Regardless of our emotions, He is able to reach us when no one else can. With God's help, we have survived some of the darkest days. Better days are ahead. I hope that by sharing our story, we are able to provide comfort to someone else along the way or bring insight to those looking for perspective. Although God did not cause this to happen, I believe He can use the worst situations to help someone else on their own journey.

-- J. Waters

Chapter 20: I am the Little Sister

I am the youngest child. I realize that most people would like to believe that life is great all around. Nobody wants to face reality and see that bad things happen, and there is nothing you can do to stop it, but that is life. Bad things do happen to good people. I am one of those people, and this is my story.

My childhood has been full of heartbreak, but not because of divorce or the loss of my parents. Instead, I lost my sister and she took a part of me. One of the worst parts about growing up was having a sister who didn't act like a sister. You see, my sister was always angry. I never knew why, but she didn't ever like me. Being the youngest, I looked up to her when I was little, but the way she behaved at home and away from home didn't add up. The older she got, the angrier she became. She was angry toward our parents and toward me, but no one knew why. She didn't know either.

She was always bossy. We fought like "normal" sisters, but one summer that all changed. Someone moved in next door. She was a little bit older than we were. She was funny and still liked to do the things I liked to do, while my sister said she was too old to play the games I liked. That's when I lost my sister. The girl who moved next door became like the big sister I never had since my sister and I hadn't ever really gotten along. Then things really went downhill.

My sister got in some trouble at school. If I told you what she did, you probably wouldn't believe me. She should have really gotten in trouble for what happened, but because she hadn't ever been in trouble at school before, it was ignored. My parents were worried about what she had done, so they made her see a counselor for help. It didn't help. It made her worse. Now she was mad at the world, and I become the target for her anger. I hadn't done anything wrong, but it wasn't long until it didn't matter what I did or didn't do, she would take everything out on me.

My sister's behavior continued to get worse. She was very moody. She was upset about something all of the time. If she didn't have something to be upset about, she would make something up or just be mad about something from a long time ago. It didn't make sense. She would blow up over the smallest things or nothing at all. We never knew what to expect from day to day. The entire family walked on egg shells. Sometimes we were all afraid, but I was always afraid. I always had been afraid of her for as long as I could remember.

Because you see, after the girl next door grew up and moved away, my sister became abusive. Now I realize that abuse takes many forms. She had been abusive my entire life, but in a different way. She always intimidated me in a lot of ways. One look said a million words that no one else realized or saw, not even our parents. Because I was afraid, I never told. Secrets aren't always a good thing. Some secrets are better told. If my parents had known the truth, the worst might not have happened. They knew I was afraid of her, but sometimes we all were. Her mood changed very quickly and we never knew what to expect. But we lived with it every day and somehow it became normal to just put up with her strange behavior.

Over time, the abuse changed from intimidation, manipulation, and threats to hurt me if she didn't get her way over little things, to sexual abuse and later violence that could have cost my life. Her abuse caused me to lose my sister forever. For a long time I blamed myself. I thought I must have done something to make her mad enough to do these things to me. Things got so bad that I couldn't live with the pain any more. Sometimes I didn't want to live. I thought that dying would be better than living with the pain, fear, and dark secrets. I didn't know what to do or where to turn. Eventually, I found a way to break the secret. I told. It was scarier than I imagined, but I hoped things would get better from there. Once my parents knew the truth, they could protect me. They would protect me. I wouldn't have to be afraid anymore. Even though this meant that my sister would always blame me for what happened to her, I would be safe, and she could get the help she needed a long time ago.

My story is proof that bad things do happen to good people. Those on the outside never know the secret things that happen behind closed doors, even when the doors are in your own house. No one should ever live in fear. By telling the secret, I chose to be safe and live.

Sometimes things are still really hard. Most people, especially people my age, don't understand what really happened or why it is difficult for me to move on. My friends ditched me. The abuse caused me to have PTSD, and it's very hard to deal with. It makes me struggle at school, and I never struggled with assignments before. Honestly, it affects every part of my life, sometimes worse than others. The symptoms of PTSD got really bad and my parents worked very hard to get me help. They even found a way to get me a service dog. She's not a pet. She helps me every day. We go everywhere together. Sometimes, she is my best friend in the whole world. I can tell her anything and she will lick away my tears and stay with me until the bad moments pass. She knows when I'm going to have a panic attack, even before I do. I try to stay positive and believe that things will get better. I try to make new friends, but sometimes they don't understand why I react to things differently than they do, or why I have panic attacks. My "uncle" bailed when I needed him most. I don't know why he walked away. Maybe he just couldn't deal with it. Maybe he didn't care as much as I thought he did. I'll never understand why he changed from a supportive person to a total stranger.

I have lost a lot. Some of those things I can never get back. I miss my "uncle," but he really isn't my uncle any more. Sometimes I wish I had a sister, a sister who would love me like a big sister should, a sister to laugh with, a sister who liked to spend time doing normal things like shopping or going to the movies. But I don't have that, and I really never did. Instead, I lost my sister long before she had to leave our house. Maybe she was lost all along in her own mind that can't think straight or see how much we all loved her. I told her once that I still love her, even though she did those horrible things to me. I told her that I would forgive her in a heartbeat, if she was ever truly sorry for what she did. And that's all true, but she isn't sorry. I'm not sure she has any feelings about what happened, other than anger that she got caught. I don't understand why she hurt me, but now I know that I didn't do anything to cause it and never deserved to be treated that way.

My parents have really had it rough through all this. Even though they have done all sorts of things for my sister to help her finish school, prepare for college, and get a job, she still acts like she hates them, especially Mom, most of the time. They pay for her cell phone and gave her a car so that she doesn't have any debt, but she doesn't appreciate it. My parents tell her they love her, but she doesn't say it back, hardly ever. She says bad things about them to other people that aren't true. She doesn't know how lucky she is to have them as parents. Things could have been very different for her, if it weren't for them.

I know I am lucky to have them as my mom and dad, because sometimes when kids tell the secret of abuse, their parents don't believe them or are afraid of what others might think, so they don't do anything to stop it from happening again. My parents are good people and are my heroes. From the moment they heard the truth, I knew I would be safe and that my sister would never hurt me again. They didn't know what to do at first, but worked hard to find answers and get help.

If you have a secret like mine, don't be afraid to tell. I know it's scary, but find a way to tell. You don't deserve abuse. Break the silence and choose life. You are worth it.

--K. Waters

Helpful Resources

Abused Women's Aid in Crisis
(907) 272-0100
www.awaic.org

Childhelp National Child Abuse Hotline
24 Hour Hotline: 1-800-422-4453
www.childhelp.org/hotline/

KidLink Treatment Centers
800-726-4032
www.kidlinknetwork.com

RAINN - Rape, Abuse and Incest National Network
24 Hour Crisis Hotline: 1-800-656-HOPE (4673)
www.rainn.org

Contact Information

If this has positively impacted your personal journey, we want to know. Don't be afraid to break the silence, whether you are the survivor of abuse, the parent of a victim and/or perpetrator, or a friend or family member struggling to help.

Follow on Facebook: SpeakOut4Hope@SarahWaters4Hope.
E-mail: speakout4hope@gmail.com
Blog: speakout4hope.wordpress.com

Made in the USA
Lexington, KY
28 November 2017